Parakeets
And
Budgies –

Raising,
Feeding,
And Hand-Training
Your Keet

Lisa Shea

~ v2 ~

Introduction

I have owned parakeets (also called budgies or keets) since I was a tiny toddler. The photo below is of my father with my mom's parakeet (named Gandalf), so she owned parakeets even before I was born. Sometimes I've owned just one parakeet, such as "Cheepie" when I was a young girl. Sometimes I've owned four parakeets and managed the ups and downs of community flocks. Through it all, I've always loved parakeets.

This book is the result of many years of research, trial, error, and discussions with other parakeet owners and lovers. I hope you enjoy the information. With it, find ways to liven up your relationship with your pet parakeet!

Parakeet FAQs

If you're not the patient sort, here are the Frequently Asked Questions, or FAQs, that most people want to know about keets.

Just What is a Parakeet?

There are lots of names for this beautiful little bird from Australia. Its scientific name is *Melopsittacus undulatus* meaning "song parrot with wavy lines." The Aborigine term for the bird was something close to "budgerigar," their phrase meaning "good to eat." They would eat budgies for snacks. The English explorers who met the aborigines and saw the birds shortened this to "budgies." Since they looked like little parrots, they're also called "parakeets" or "keets" for short. A lot of names for a little bird!

What is a Budgie Like?

Budgies are friendly, easy to train, might learn to talk, and are flock animals. They either need a human around all the time or some parakeet flockmates. They live from seven to fifteen years if taken care of well and are not breeding. Some have even been known to live to twenty years or more.

Why do some Budgies die Earlier?

Many budgies which die before age five are poorly fed and die of malnutrition. There is also a window of time where a budgie might develop a tumor. If a parakeet starts acting poorly around age five to seven it is probably a tumor. Take your bird to a vet if you notice its breastbone sticking out or that the bird has trouble sitting on its perch.

If your bird makes it through this period it will probably live a long life and die of old age.

What do Parakeets Eat?

In essence the parakeet in its native Australian grasslands would eat a variety of foods. Yes, in the fall they ate the grass seed. But they also ate the fresh greens of the grasses, the fruits and berries they found, plus some protein material as well. A healthy budgie needs a balanced diet.

How do I tell a Male from a Female?

The easiest way on an adult is to look at the bump of flesh above its nose - the "cere." On a male this is blueish. On a female this is brownish. Males tend to be more likely to talk. Females love to gnaw, because one of their primary tasks in the Eucalyptus groves of their homeland was to gnaw out a nest for the baby keets. The cuttlebones you put into their cages serve not only as a good beak-trimming tool, but also a great gnawing spot.

Why does my Parakeet Spit Up Food?

This is the ultimate compliment a parakeet can give. When a mommy parakeet is sitting on her eggs, sometimes the father will bring her food in this way. He can't really bring food in his claws, so he eats it, comes back to her and then regurgitates it so she can have some. Also, this is how the mommy parakeet feeds her babies. She doesn't have teats that give milk. Instead, she cats a food, lets it digest a bit in her stomach, then regurgitates it in a nice, soft format so the babies can eat it easily. If your parakeet is regurgitating food for you, it is the parakeet's way of saying he loves you.

My Parakeet is Picking at His Feathers

A parakeet will normally preen his feathers daily, keeping them clean and free of dust. So you might see your parakeet sliding his feathers through his beak, nibbling at his feathers, scratching his head with his claws, and fluffing up. This is all normal. If you find your parakeet is actually yanking out feathers repeatedly (or yanking out one of his flockmate's feathers) it's time to talk to a vet.

How do Parakeets Sleep?

Parakeets need a solid ten to twelve hours of sleep a day. The bulk of this is at night, when you should put a cover on the cage so they feel safe. In nature, they would tuck into a hole in a tree and be surrounded by bark. They also take naps during the day. Sometimes they just close their eyes. Sometimes they raise one foot (like a flamingo) to give it some rest. Sometimes they tuck their head on their back wing so give their neck a rest.

Do Parakeets Pee?

What a funny question! Actually parakeets do not really pee. When they have to go, they make little round poops that are grey on the outside and white in the center. These hold both the liquid and solid wastes in sort of a pudding-like consistency. They're small and odorless, and you just change the cage paper weekly to remove them.

Allergies and Diseases

Sure, you could be allergic to parakeets. People can be allergic to newsprint, peanuts, Styrofoam, you name it. Only you know what you are allergic to. But most people aren't allergic to parakeets. As far as diseases go, it's not like your parakeet is roaming the woods to "catch something." You should *always* take any new pet to a vet to get a check-up and make sure it starts out healthy. But if a vet says it is healthy, the chance of it mysteriously catching something while it sits in a room in your house is slim to none. And since you live in that house too, chances are you are the one who gave that disease to your pet!

Laws and Banding

Most states and many countries now have their laws online to search through. I have a summary of US laws on my website to help you out. As far as I can tell, the only state that requires leg bands is Virginia, and that's only for monk / Quaker parakeets.

What Temperature Range do Budgies Need?

Wild budgies live in the central area of Australia - in hot, dry deserts. Summertime temperatures get into the mid to high 90s. The budgies hide in the trees during the day, and try to stay cool. In the winter they migrate to stay in a warm zone, usually not below 68-70F. In a cage, since they are "trapped" at the temperature you set and cannot escape to a warmer or cooler spot, make sure to keep the temperatures in the middle - around 70-80F. Always have water available so they can cool down, and if there is sunlight or light shining into the cage, always have a shady spot where they can retreat to.

A History of Budgies

Birds have been kept as pets since the days of the Egyptians. They have always been treasured for their beautiful colors, their lovely voices, and their friendliness.

Australia's dry grasslands have been home to the *Melopsittacus undulatus* for thousands of years. The Native Aborigines would watch huge flocks of these green songbirds rise over the plains, observing as the birds stayed near groves of eucalyptus trees and built their nests in the holes of the trees. The Aborigines would often use their boomerangs, throwing the weapons into the center of the flock of keets to take out a few for a snack. Yes, the English word "budgerigar," by which this bird is known, comes from the Australian phrase "good to eat."

Since they look very much like tiny parrots, the nickname for these birds is "parakeet," or "keet" for short. The Latin name translates to "song parrot with wavy lines." The black, wavy lines on the back of a parakeet, over the green feathers, helped keep it hidden in the green grasslands of its native Australia.

In 1838, John Gould, a naturalist, traveled to Australia and brought two parakeets back home with him to England. The birds were quite friendly and amazingly easy to breed. In only a few short years there were thousands of parakeets all over Europe and their popularity was skyrocketing. By 1894 the Australians were worried about the vast numbers of budgies being trapped and banned all export of the cute little bird. That ban is still in effect today. Any budgie that you buy has been raised by breeders, probably within a short radius of your home.

There are currently around 8 million parakeets in the United States, with many millions more in the rest of the world. Budgies are enjoyed in just about every country of the world, and are perfect pets for young and old alike. They are easy to care for, very friendly, and relatively inexpensive. According to bird researchers, parakeets are in the top five of intelligent pet birds!

How Parakeets Look

Parakeets were originally found in huge flocks in Australia's central grassland plains. In their native lands, parakeets were all green in color, with black wavy bands on their wings and backs. This combination helped them to be camouflaged in the grassy plains and eucalyptus trees which were their homes.

When parakeet ownership took off in the mid-1800s, suddenly people wanted to see what breeding could do for the parakeet. By mating the right combinations of parents, breeders could bring out certain colors in the bird's children. This is normal 'breeding' behavior that pet owners do with dogs, cats, cows, sheep, horses, and pretty much any other animal.

For example, breeders could encourage birds that were bluer to mate with each other, causing their children to become even more blue. Then the more-blue parakeets would mate, creating babies that were even bluer.

The result is that today we have many different colors of parakeets. Blue is the second most common color for parakeets, because it is the color closest to green is blue. So that was the easiest color for breeders to achieve.

There are also:

* Purple parakeets
* Light Blue parakeets
* White parakeets
* Parakeets with white spots
* Parakeets with multiple colors

    Green is still the most commonly found color and is its "normal" color.
    The color of a parakeet doesn't really matter - it's all up to the buyer which color he or she enjoys the most.

Lisa Shea

Parakeet Sounds and Vocalizations

Parakeets are very smart creatures and are used to living in gigantic flocks with thousands of members. They would use a variety of calls and chirps to stay in contact with each other, to warn of danger, to track down their children, and much more. These same noises and chirps are used when they are pets in your cage!

Note that while other parrots can be quite loud - including cockatiels and macaws - parakeets are not extremely loud. If you neglect them they may cry out for attention, but if you take good care of them, they will be peaceful and happy!

Contented Warble
The most common sound heard by most good parakeet owners is the contented warble. Parakeets do this while they are falling asleep, while they are listening to music, hanging out on your shoulder, preening themselves. This is sort of like a cat purring.

General Fweeping
Parakeets love music and will sing along with songs as best they can by fweeping merrily. They won't normally just spontaneously do this if it's quiet, but if there's music playing they'll add in their own voices. Note that if you leave your parakeets alone you should leave some music playing to keep them company. In the wild, there was always noise. If there was NOT noise it was a sign that there was a predator lurking around. So to leave your parakeets in a dead silent area is going to give them a lot of stress.

Ack-Ack-Ack
Remember the movie *Mars Attacks*? Every parakeet owner I know say that the Ack-Ack is a form of Parakeet Talk. It's sort of a parakeet's way of saying "Hah hah!" or "Look at this!" or "I'm so excited and I just can't hide it!" :)

13

Parakeets

ARK! ARK! ARK!
Where ack-ack-ack! is a light, cheery cry that usually involves the parakeet bobbing its head up and down in sheer abandon, there's a separate cry that it makes when for example a flockmate is trying to pull her tail out. This is a loud angry ARK! ARK! ARK! which is a STOP IT RIGHT NOW YOU JERK!!! call.

High Pitched Yelp / FWEEP
This is a cry of distress. With our three parakeets, if one of them gets separated from the other two it will begin to yelp. This is sort of a "Lost! Lost!" cry, and the other parakeets will all out to it to help it find its way back home again. In fact, sometimes if Bob leaves the room after being in there for a while, the other parakeets will assume he's "lost" and start yelping for him, to help him get back to the safe home. He has to go back and tell them he's OK, that he's just going to be away for a little while, and they settle down. We call this their "FWEEP!" :)

Human Speech
You can teach your parakeet to talk if you're patient and your parakeet is interested in learning. Male parakeets are easier to teach than females, and young parakeets that were hand raised are the easiest to teach. Don't worry if your parakeet doesn't learn to talk, not all do. Your parakeet will still be able to communicate to you in its own warbles and fweeps.

Other Noises
Parakeets are very smart and love making interesting sounds. So parakeets learn to make noises like cell phones ringing, trucks backing up, or whatever other sounds they hear in their environment. My parakeets don't talk, but I've taught them to sing "Fee-Bee" like a chickadee, with the first note high and the second note low. They love that, and it drives the chickadees outside crazy :)

Regular Parakeet vs English Budgie

As parakeets have become hugely popular, they become birds that are often seen at bird shows. A certain "look" of parakeet became the best judged parakeets at these shows - a parakeet with a big body and big head.

Because most show-winners were from England, this style of parakeet became known as the "English Budgie." It's not that an English Budgie is really any different from a regular budgie. All it means is that the bird is a larger size bird. It's sort of like calling a tall human being a "Basketball Human" just because he's tall. An English Budgie is just a larger, specially bred parakeet who had big parents

Monk Parakeet / Quaker Parakeet

The Monk Parakeet, also called the Quaker Parakeet, originally comes from South America. It is found in Brazil, Bolivia, Argentina, Paraguay and Uruguay. This is different from the "standard" parakeet, which comes from Australia. Monk parakeets are a little larger than a standard parakeet and are kept as pets for much the same reason that traditional parakeets are - because they are easy to care for, fun to play with and very intelligent.

Interestingly, because Monk Parakeets come from mountainous regions of South America, they can survive in most of the US, even through the winter. Over the years many monk parakeets have escaped from homes, and entire boxes of them being shipped up from South America have broken open by accident. Where regular parakeets would have been eaten and/or died, the Monk Parakeets have survived and created wild colonies in various locations of the US.

Because they survive so easily in the wild and can pose a huge hazard for crops, Monk Parakeets are illegal to own in these states:

* California
* Wyoming
* New Jersey
* Hawaii
* Georgia

Monk parakeets are usually green with grey feathers, and can live up to 35 years.

Average prices for monk parakeets start at $150-$200.

This copyright-free image of a Monk Parakeet was supplied by Lip Kee Yap –

Rose-ringed Parakeet / Hawaiian Parakeet

The Rose-ringed Parakeet, or ring-necked parakeet (*Psittacula krameri*), is originally found in Africa and parts of Asia. They are naturally green in color, with distinctive red beaks. They have a black ring around their necks, and are around 17 inches long. As bird breeders tend to do, they have now created ringed parakeets in other colors. The colors are almost always solid colors, without the 'shell pattern' typical on budgies.

Rose-ringed parakeets are sometimes called a Hawaiian parakeet because they were introduced to those islands and now live there in the wild. They have also established colonies in England, Florida and California.

Rose-ringed parakeets are very noisy and have a tendency to squawk loudly.

Copyright-free image supplied by Hafiz Issadeen.

Carolina Parakeet - Extinct

The Carolina Parakeet was the only parakeet native to North America. It lived a peaceful life until the 1800s, when man began taking over the landscape with farms. The Carolina parakeet thought this was dandy and began living off the giant bounty of food provided. Farmers did not like this at all and treated the Carolina parakeet as a nuisance, much as they treat ravens and crows.

While the Carolina Parakeet once covered much of southeastern US, soon it was the subject of widespread attempts to wipe it out. Unfortunately, the farmers were successful. The last Carolina parakeets were seen in Florida in the 1880s, and it is now extinct.

This image was done by John James Audubon.

Preparing for your New Parakeet

I know it's tempting to buy your parakeet, cage, food, and everything else in a wild rush. Resist! Make sure you get the cage and everything perfectly set up before you shop for the keet. Then bring the keet home so you can immediately put her into her new home. Otherwise she'll be stuck in her tiny travel box for a long time while you get everything else set. That'll be traumatic!

Take your time researching cages, food options, cuttlebones, and everything else you'll need. Make sure it sets up well in the area you had intended. Get it all just right. Then go and bring your new playmate home.

The following pages will get you started on creating the ideal parakeet world for your new pet.

Budgie Cages

One of the most important decisions you can make for your parakeet is the cage he or she lives in. This cage is their safe retreat, their home, their comfort spot. A parakeet is a flock creature that was meant to fly the wide open grasslands of Australia, living high in eucalyptus trees. If you try to squash this bird into a tiny cage, the bird will be miser- able and unhappy, and probably not last very long.

Get the biggest cage you can afford. Really. Your parakeet needs to be able to hop- fly from perch to perch to get some exercise when they can't be out enjoying the room. The cage bars should be close enough together that the bird's head can't fit through them. A typical restriction is that they should be 1/2" apart or less.

There shouldn't be any tiny angles or curly metal pieces that might catch a parakeet's toes or other body parts. A drawbridge-opening entrance is great because it allows the parakeet to land on it when returning home. If you don't have a drawbridge- door, consider using a rope perch outside your cage to create that landing area. You can see that on the photo of the cage below.

Put a variety of wood and rope perches into the cage. You want the parakeet's feet to have different textures and different sized perches to grab onto, so the feet get some exercise. Parakeets love to gnaw and these will also give your parakeet something to chew on. Do not use gravel-covered perches. Those rip open the tender feet of the parakeet!

Put in a few parakeet toys. Birds love bells, ropes, and hoops. If you use bells, don't use the Christmas-bell types with tiny openings. Bird feet can get caught in these. Use the Liberty-bell type ones with a bit opening at the bottom and a clapper. Rotate your toys every few months. Parakeets are very smart and will get bored with a toy after a while.

Line the bottom of the cage with paper and change it every week. Don't use gravel paper - again, when your parakeets walk down there, you don't want their feet to be ripped open. You'll need a cage cover of some sort for Parakeet Sleep Time.

Cage Location

Once you've chosen the perfect cage for your budgie or parakeet, it's important to place it in an area that is well suited for your parakeet to stay healthy and happy. Here are some guidelines to follow.

Temperature Control

Parakeets are originally from the Australian grasslands. This means they lived life in temperate weather. This wasn't the broiling desert - but neither was it the frigid arctic. You want your budgies to be at normal house temperature - between 65F and 85F - without having any giant fluctuations on a day to day basis. Be sure to keep breezes away from your budgies, especially at night. Budgie cages should be covered at night so they feel safe and secure, and the cover will help keep them warm, too.

Near People

Budgies are flock creatures and are used to living in massive clouds of birds, over 1,000 strong, in the wild. They get incredibly lonely if they're kept all alone, all day! Put your budgie in the most commonly used room in the house, and interact with him often. If you aren't around all day, get your budgie a friend to keep him company. In the wild, silence was a sign of danger - that all creatures were hiding because a predator was near. If you leave your budgie alone in the quiet, she will go stir crazy!

Keep the Cage High

Budgies like to be up high. It makes them feel safe, that they can look down at their surroundings. When pet keets fly around free, they tend to land on curtain rods to feel like the King of their Domain. Keep the cage at a level that you can easily change the food and water, but definitely put it as high as you can. Your parakeets will appreciate it!

There are many types of cage supports and hangers. You can hang your cage from a solid hook in the ceiling, hang it from a metal hook or put it on a shelf. If you're hanging the cage, make very sure the hangar is solid and cannot pull out. A simple hook into the wall will not do - you need an anchor to hold it in place. If the cage rests on a shelf or table, and you have pets, make sure there is no ledge on the side where the pet can sit next to the cage.

Humidity Levels for a Parakeet

If you're new to parakeets, you might not think twice about humidity levels. Humidity is for tropical plants, right? Yes, that's true - but humidity is also very important for your little keet or budgie.

First, what is humidity? Humidity is the amount of moisture that is in the air. If the air gets very dry, your fingers and nose can crack from the dryness. Humans put lotion on their hands. You can't do that with keets!

You can find humidity meters - just like thermometers measure temperature - in most pet stores and Walmart type stores. they are only $3-$5 for a basic humidity meter. They will give you the percent humidity. At pet stores, humidity meters are often found in the reptile area, since it's very important for reptiles to stay moist.

For keets, if it's too dry it can cause their nose and feet to crack and even bleed. It can cause other dehydration problems as well.

Once you get a humidity meter, you want to aim for between 60% to 70% humidity. If you are lower than that, it's time to get a humidifier for the room. These devices take water from a reservoir and send it out into the air. Not only will it make your keets feel better and more healthy, but it'll be good for the humans too! Everyone needs proper humidity to thrive.

If you have the opposite problem - too *much* humidity - then you can get issues with mold and bacteria. That would be the time to get a dehumidifier. These devices draw water out of the air and into a reservoir.

If you have to use either type of a device, put it on the opposite end of the room as the parakeet cage. You don't want a breeze blowing at a parakeet, perhaps giving them a chill.

For those who like fun facts, the technical term for a meter that measures humidity is a hygrometer.

Cage Liner / Cage Bottom

When Parakeets have to go to the bathroom, they create a round 'poop' that is grey on the outside and white on the inside. It's only 1/4" across or less, very small. These are semi-moist and dry very quickly. They don't really smell at all and just gather on the bottom of the cage, on the newspaper that you put at the bottom to collect these.

Once a week or so you need to throw away that old newspaper and put in some new newspaper. That keeps your parakeet's world clean and free from disease or trouble.

A healthy parakeet's poop will be semi-firm and they will poop several times a day.

If your parakeet doesn't poop at all for an entire day, talk to a vet to try to figure out what could be wrong. If your parakeet's poops are extremely watery and don't hold that circle shape, talk to a vet too. Sometimes if your keet gorges on fresh lettuce and such the poop can get *slightly* watery and green, which is normal. But a stool that's too watery can also be a sign of illness.

Cleaning a Parakeet Cage

Keeping a parakeet cage clean is critical for your parakeets' long term health. It's very important that you keep their home - their bedroom, kitchen, living room and dining room - clean and fresh.

First, there should be a cage liner in the bottom of the cage, to catch poops. Newspaper works really well for this, and generally you have some around the house for free! Don't worry about keets eating it - it's quite safe for them. Replace that at least once a week.

About once a month, take out all the toys, perches and grates that might be at the bottom. Give these a good scrubbing with water, baking soda and a mild detergent if you wish. The baking soda will provide "grit" to help scrub off hard bits without endangering the keets at all.

Every six months or so it's good to hose down the entire cage. Of course the keets need to be hand trained by this point - because they're going to be out of the cage! Take the cage outside or into the bathroom, and rinse it down completely inside and out. Remember that a keet is going to be gnawing on pretty much everything in the cage - so don't use any harsh detergents, Windex, Fantastic, or anything like that. Just use water and a mild detergent if you have to. Let it all thoroughly dry before you put the keet back in.

Do Parakeets Stink / Smell?

Many people are curious if parakeets smell. It's sort of asking if dogs smell. You can have a dog that is kept clean and has pretty much no odor at all. You can also have a dog that is never washed, that rolls around in the mud all day, and that has an *incredible* stench. It is all up to you.

In general, parakeets do not smell at all! They are very clean creatures. If you give them a bathtub, they will gladly take baths every day. They preen themselves constantly. They don't go outside. They don't go in the mud. They don't really "get dirty". They eat dried seeds and fresh fruits and veggies. They don't have bad breath. They are some of the cleanest animals out there.

Does a keet cage smell? Well, I suppose it does if you don't clean it. Keet poops are very tiny and are small, dry circles. They really don't smell at all. Still, if you let those poops pile up for months, they would start to stink. If you clean the cage properly, there won't be a smell associated with them. You want to keep the cage clean, for regular sanitary issues!

Their food is usually dried pellets or dried seed. Those have no odor at all. You also feed the keets fresh fruits and veggies. I suppose those smell like fresh fruits and veggies - apple, orange, etc. But you give them the food, and when they're done eating, you take it away. So it only has that aroma while they're eating. It's like when you sit down to dinner, the table smells like the food you're eating. Then when you wash the plates, that aroma goes away. You don't feed your parakeets garlic or fish :). So they're not eating smelly foods.

So in general, a keet is a very odor free pet, if cared for properly!

Air Conditioning

If your room is hot, use air conditioning.

Think of it this way. What if the normal temperature was 110F? Your parakeets would roast. Air conditioning does its job to make a comfortable temperature that is better for healthy living. That's why we humans use it. Sometimes fans just can't help.

That being said, be sure to not direct the air stream at them. You want the parakeets in a comfortable, stable environment.

If you are worried about the gas in the AC unit, that never gets out. It's only regular air that comes out - it is cooled by touching cooled items inside the unit. Also, hospitals are cooled by AC so I think if there was ever a serious risk to babies and elderly and such that it's long since been addressed.

So, to summarize, it's far more important to keep your keets from overheating than to worry about any risk of the gas within the air conditioner harming a parakeet.

Winter Heating

Parakeets are tropical birds. In the wild they live on the grasslands of Australia, hanging out in trees, soaring in the sky, enjoying the sunshine. The average temperature ranges between 60F and 80F. Remember that keets in the wild are able to seek shade if they need to, and do not have drastic changes where it goes from 80F to 60F instantly. While they can fluff their feathers up to stay warm, they were simply not meant for freezing cold temperatures. They are not penguins!

This can pose a problem for individuals who live in very cold, drafty houses. Both the cold temperature and the sharp breezes can cause damage to a parakeet's health. While a human can put on snuggly pajamas and pile quilts on top of them, a parakeet is stuck!

Here are some ideas for keeping your parakeet safe and warm in the winter.

Thermometer

You won't know how cold it gets without a thermometer. They have cheap $2 thermometers at Walmart and other stores that have a "minimum memory". That is, if it gets down to 50F overnight, it will show you that minimum 50F value as one of its readings when you wake up the next morning even if the temperature has gone back up to 60F by then. It's really important to have a thermometer that tracks minimum values. That way you always know "how bad" it gets in the dead of night, and can take steps to fix the problem if there is one.

Bird Snugglie

There are many "fuzzy bird tubes" out there that birds can go into and sleep in. The trick here is if your bird will actually go into it. Birds are very unique and one bird might adore a bird tube while another might hate it with a passion. If your room is cold, it might at least be worth a try. Put some yummy millet into the tube and give your bird a few weeks to get used to it. Your keet might be afraid of it at first, but over time your keet might adore sleeping in it. Then again, your keet might simply decide she hates it. It is all up to your bird's unique mentality!

Part of the benefit, if your bird does adapt to a bird snugglie, is that they can go in and out based on their own needs. So they can warm up or cool down on their own schedule.

Cage Cover

The first step for keeping out breezes and drafts, and to provide some insulation for the keet, would be a heavy blanket to put over the cage at night. Just like a tent keeps you warm when you camp, a blanket will provide a barrier against breezes and allow the air within the cage to stay still. This means the keet's body - as small as it is - can warm up that air and keep it slightly warmer than it might be otherwise. It's like a big sleeping bag, in essence. If you're not currently covering your keet's cage at night, this is an important first step.

Heating pad

You might think that heat rises - but actually cold air falls! Cold air is denser than warm air, so when air warms up, the cold air above it is too heavy to stay up there and heads down. Over time it keeps going down, leaving only warm air in the area. The key here is again to cover the cage first - and put a heating pad beneath the cage. That way as the cold air sinks, the warm air stays within the cage, keeping your keet warm.

Of course make sure you use a safe heating pad. You don't want to set your keet on fire! Make sure there is no way for the keet to get her beak on the pad or wires to chew on them. Keets love to chew, of course, and you don't want your keet anywhere near something with electricity in it.

Homemade Heating Pad

If you want to have a cheap version, I have a "neck warmer" which is simply a sock of cloth filled up with hard rice. You simply microwave it for a minute or so and it says warm for a half hour. You can do the same thing for your keets, make a pillow of rice and use your microwave to warm it up. As always, make sure it is not *too* hot before you put it near your keets.

Window Covers

The way many rooms get cold is that cold air works its way in through windows. Something I did at many chilly apartments was to seal the windows with plastic as soon as winter approached. You tape the plastic around all edges of the window. It is *amazing* how much warmer the room stays. You save tens if not hundreds of dollars in heating costs. You can buy the plastic very cheaply at many stores, and you easily save that money in just a few weeks. This is good not only for your keet's health but for your own as well.

Thick Curtains

Even if you do plastic coat your windows, always have thick curtains. You can get cheap, heavy fabric from a store and make your own! The heavy curtains can definitely make a big difference in retaining heat at night.

Door Blocks

Cold air is notorious for seeping down along the base of doors. Make some snakes in the same way you make a heating pad - with a "sock" of cloth filled with rice. Line the bottoms of your doors with them. You'll be amazed at how well it helps to control drafts.

Room Heaters

Be very careful with in-room heaters that radiate heat. Some of these can get quite hot, and if your keet gets loose she could get burned and seriously injured. If this ends up being a necessary step for you, be sure to research the heater options carefully and to supervise your keet with great caution when she is out of the cage.

Healthy Food

The native parakeet grew up in the grasslands of Australia, living in eucalyptus trees. Those grasslands provided the parakeets what they needed to live. They would eat the fresh greens, the fruits and berries they found there, and the seeds that came in the fall.

So while parakeet seed is *one* part of what a parakeet's diet should have in it, it is definitely not *all*, and a parakeet raised solely on parakeet seed will have some form of malnutrition. Even the fortified seeds you find in stores are usually fortified with a pow- der sprinkled on the outside of the seed. Since a parakeet hulls its seeds before eating them, leaving behind that outer shell, the fortification does little good.

Below is a photo (a bit fuzzy, I admit) of typical parakeet seed. It offers a few different shapes and sizes for the parakeet to nibble on. Seed is fine as a start, but it is *not* enough. What if *you* tried to live on just white bread? You'd miss a ton of nutrients.

Your parakeet is the exact same way.

The Association of Avian Veterinarians recommends the following diet for a parakeet:

* 50% cooked beans, whole wheat bread, cooked rice, pasta, and seed

* 45% fresh broccoli, carrots, yams, spinach, dandelion greens, other green/orange fruits and veggies

* 5% eggs, tuna packed in water, well cooked meat

Overfeeding a Parakeet

Parakeets do *not* overeat. If anything, people tend to give them too little food, thinking a seed cup is full when really it's just full of the hulls of the seeds the parakeet has already eaten. Be sure to refill your parakeet's food supply daily and to give him or her lots of fresh foods too.

Healthy Food by Vitamin

It's very important for you to feed your parakeet a healthy combination of foods. A parakeet's eyes can see the freshness of food, so if something looks old and icky to you, don't feed it to your keet!

Here are the important things to feed to your budgie.

Vitamin	Foods
Vitamin A	alfalfa, broccoli, carrots, egg yolks, spinach, zucchini
Vitamin B	asparagus, broccoli, eggs, nuts
Vitamin C	asparagus, broccoli, potatoes, zucchini
Vitamin D	egg yolk and sunlight
Vitamin E	alfalfa, egg yolk, spinach
Vitamin K	alfalfa, spinach
Calcium	broccoli, dandelion, kale, mineral block
Protein	beans, chicken, corn, fish, turkey

Healthy Water

Be sure your parakeet always has fresh water. Water is *critical* for a healthy parakeet. IT has to be clean. *You* would not drink water out of your toilet bowl with poop floating in it, would you?? Your parakeet is just as much a clean freak as you are - if not more so!

You should change your parakeet's water daily. Parakeets (and all other living creatures for that matter) enjoy fresh water. Water that sits still for a while gets stagnant, scummy and slimy. Nobody likes to drink scummy water.

Make sure you keep the water dish up high where it won't have things falling into it.

This can include seed hulls, feathers, millet, or other such things. Sometimes the occasional feather will drift in anyway, but again if you're changing the water daily, it shouldn't matter much.

Don't put any supplements or other items into the water. Some salesmen try to get you to buy 'liquid vitamins' that you put into your bird's water to super-nutrient the bird. Those vitamins can make the water taste funny, so now the bird isn't drinking the water at all and gets sick. The vitamins also promote bacterial growth, which can also make your bird sick.

Dangerous Foods

Chocolate

Parakeets are HIGHLY allergic to chocolate. Chocolate isn't great for humans to gobble up either, but at least we don't die from it. Parakeets (and dogs and many other pets) have nasty reactions to chocolate and can literally die if fed it. Keep the chocolate FAR away from your parakeets. Never leave it out anywhere that a parakeet might find it.

Avocados

Avocados are another food that are highly toxic for many pets. If you enjoy avocados, be sure to do so in a very safe manner, far from your budgies.

Junk Food

Junk food such as pretzels, potato chips, etc. are pretty bad for you as a human, with the trans fatty acids and other nasty preservatives in them. Parakeets have *very* small bodies and even a small dose of toxin can kill them. It is really best to keep all junk foods away from them.

Apple / Cherry Seeds

It of course is important for your keet to get some
fresh fruit in their diet. You can feed a parakeet fresh
fruit such as apples and cherries, but be careful about
the seeds as those have toxins in them. Thoroughly
search the chunks of fruit for seeds before giving them
to the budgies.

Lettuce

Lettuce is fine in the sense that it won't harm your
parakeet. But as far as having meaningful vitamins,
lettuce – especially iceberg lettuce - really has no
nutrients in it. It's better to give your budgies other,
healthier greens such as spinach. The more 'empty
calories' the budgie fills his or her stomach up with,
the less space that will be left for the foods they *should*
be eating.

Milk and Dairy Products

Just like most adult humans, parakeets are lactose-
tolerant. This means their tummies cannot properly
digest milk and dairy products. Therefore, while small
nibbles are fine, do not feed your parakeets a lot of
dairy product.

Dangerous Plants

The following plants are poisonous and should be kept away from parakeets. It's really safest not to keep them *anywhere* in the house, as parakeets are notorious for flying where they should not belong :).

Amaryllis
calla lily
daffodil
English ivy
foxglove
holly
lily of the valley
mistletoe
rhubarb

VERY IMPORTANT
If you have a parakeet, it's best to rid your house of non-stick cookware. If you *ever* accidentally leave one of these pots or pans on the stove and it runs dry, the odors put off from the cookware are fatal to parakeets. It's far safer to not have any in the house than to take that chance.

I've had this happen to dear friends of mine, and it's quite tragic.

Overfeeding a Parakeet

Unlike many humans I know, parakeets do *not* naturally tend to overeat :). If any- thing, people tend to give them too little food, thinking a seed cup is full when really it's just full of the hulls of the seeds the parakeet has already eaten. So most owners I know end up with parakeets who are starving by the time the next seed dish is put into the cage.

However, I have read a pellet food maker's recommendation recently that you only serve your parakeets 2 Tablespoons of pellets every day. 1 Tablespoon in the morning, 1 tablespoon in the evening. The maker says that this makes your parakeet "really hungry" before the pellets get there, so the parakeet really enjoys the food.

I respect that every one of us has his or her own opinion on life - but I know that with *humans*, people used to be told to only eat three times a day and not snack in between. This was supposedly "healthy". But what they found was that hungry humans were cranky humans. The body didn't like having energy in a big dose, then no energy at all at other times. The body went through high-low swings, it wreaked havoc with the body, with the happiness. Nowadays nutritionists recommend that people eat those three meals, but also have regular food and water as snacks (*healthy* snacks) at other times. You should never go more than 2-3 hours without a snack. That keeps your body on an even keel.

The argument that you can only really enjoy food when you're starving to death is nonsense, as far as I'm concerned. In my experience, when you're starving to death, you hardly savor the flavor of what you're eating! Instead, you jam it into your mouth quickly because you have a basic body danger situation going on. The same is true with keets. When you feed a starving parakeet, they aren't savoring their food's flavors. They are jamming food into their stomach as fast as they can, because they finally got their needs met.

And the fact that you stress your parakeet every day for a basic necessity can't be good. Your parakeet has to trust you as an owner, that you'll take proper care of them. But how can they trust you if they sit there waiting and hoping and praying that you get to them before the pain in their stomach gets unbearable? That would be like thinking it's great to stress a dog out every night by not taking him for a walk until his bladder is about to explode. How is deliberately adding negative stress into a pet's life a good thing?

I do have to say that some people fill their parakeet's stomachs with *unhealthy* food. If all you do all day is feed your parakeet sugar, your parakeet is going to end up fat and malnourished. This isn't because your parakeet is eating too much. This is because your parakeet is not eating *healthy food*. She is filling her stomach on sugary things, not having room to eat healthy things, and malnutrition results. So it is your responsibility to ensure that your parakeet gets the healthy foods before the treats.

Remember, your parakeet is like a human toddler. If you put out in front of a human toddler a bunch of plates, and one with candy on it, the toddler would go for that candy and eat it all up if she could. Your parakeet is the same way. So save millet and sweet foods for special occasions - and make the regular foods healthy ones.

Dealing with a Picky Eater

Parakeets are just like picky toddlers - they get used to eating whatever they are fed and then demand it daily, even if other interesting (and more nutritious!) things are out there in the world. You need to take this slowly and patiently. You definitely don't want your parakeet to starve to death because he or she is afraid of the new foods you try to provide!

The trick is to appeal to the innate curiosity of a parakeet. Parakeets are incredibly smart and can learn the names of things, so they certainly understand when some- thing is yummy. They are also very much of a "MINE! MINE! MINE!" mentality and if they see you have something that looks like fun, they want to have some too.

Parakeets also love to gnaw, so anything that looks fun and involves gnawing on something appeals to them. You just have to get them over their natural nervousness of strange things.

With my parakeets, Nazo is always the "brave" one, but there's no way Pinto or Santo would just spontaneously eat something new I put in their cage. It is too scary. So what I do is put Nazo on my finger, where she's happy and content. Then I take a piece of say lettuce and start nibbling on it. I don't push it in her face, but I have it where she can see it. I make happy noises (Yummmmm!) when I eat it.

After a little while of this, Nazo gets intrigued. At this point I can start moving the lettuce closer to her. Again, I don't force it on her, but as I nibble away, she will reach over and try to nibble some too. Parakeets love lettuce so this is a good one to start with. After a few times of doing this, she'll leap for it with delight when I bring it around.

Once you get your parakeet eating lettuce, move on to a few other vegetables, one at a time. Don't just leave it in the cage and hope that your parakeet will realize it's food.

Don't force your parakeet to eat only the new food, your parakeet might choose to starve rather than risk poisoning herself with something unknown. You have to train your parakeet that this new object is edible and tasty.

Remember, parakeets *do have tongues*. They have a sense of taste. Different parakeets like different things. Some parakeets love carrots. Some hate them. Some love tomatoes. Some hate them. Keep going through different fruits and vegetables and learn what *your* parakeet likes and dislikes. A parakeet journal is invaluable in this effort.

Soon you'll have your keet eating a complete, nutritious diet! Be sure to read the information on what foods to avoid, though. There are some foods that parakeets can't tolerate well!

Kibble and Pellets

Just like most people feed their cats and dogs "kibble" (processed pellets) instead of their natural foods (rabbits, rats, etc.) some people also feed their parakeets "kibble."

Parakeet kibble is nutritionally balanced and a great way to meet all of the parakeet's food requirements easily. It is fortified with vitamins, nicely crunchy/chewy, and comes in a variety of flavors.

Some parakeets love kibble, just like some cats love dried cat food. However, other parakeets are convinced they want to eat "real food" with a variety of textures, flavors, and taste sensations. Think of this in your own life. What if you were only fed crunchy, dried pellets for food 24 hours a day, 7 days a week. Wouldn't you get bored of it after a while?

I have to admit that I've never converted any of my parakeets to a kibble-only diet.

I've tried a number of times. The way you do it is by mixing it in slowly. If you just take out the old food and only put in kibble, your parakeets won't know what to make of it - and they could have serious malnutrition issues if they stop eating for a while during the conversion process. So instead, most brands recommend:

First week - 3/4 the old food, 1/4 the new kibble, mixed together.
Second week - 1/2 the old food, 1/2 the new kibble, mixed together.
Third week - 1/4 the old food, 3/4 the new kibble, mixed together.
Fourth week - only new kibble.

Most kibbles recommend around 2 Tbsp kibble per bird, per day. In general parakeets will not overeat so it's usually safer to put out more than necessary to ensure they get enough food.

Whichever way you go, be sure to give your parakeet a diet that is balanced and healthy. If you feed kibble, supplement with a few fruits and vegetables so at least the bird gets some variety in his diet. If you feed seed, be sure to also include the fruits, vegetables, and other grains that make up a balanced parakeet diet.

Millet - a Parakeet Treat

You'll find millet in many pet stores. Millet is in essence seed stalks where the seeds were dried right on the stalks. In this photo, the millet spray is on the left, and regular 'parakeet seed' is on the right.

Millet is very high in fat and is a *treat* for parakeets. It should only be fed to them occasionally. Parakeets in the wild certainly did not have millet year-round!

Parakeet Eating Poop

As humans we are trained that eating poop is a bad thing. However, for animals such as parakeets, eating poop is simply a way to try to get vitamins or minerals they are lacking in their normal diet. The parakeet cannot go to the store and buy different food. They have to try to do the best with what is available to them in their cage.

The technical term for this behavior is *coprophagia*. Some creatures, like rabbits, do this as part of their natural cycle. By giving food two passes through their stomach they get as many nutrients as possible from their food.

Parakeets normally don't need to eat their poop. They should get adequate nutrition from the mixture of seed, vegetables, calcium blocks, and other food items supplied to them. However, if a pet owner is not providing the parakeet with a full range of nutritional items - for example restricting their parakeet to a seed only diet - then a variety of malnutrition issues can arise. The parakeet will resort to things such as eating her own poop in an effort to survive.

The most common nutritional deficiency to cause a parakeet to eat her own poop is a lack of proper minerals. Make sure you have a cuttlebone and a mineral block in your cage in a location where the keet can easily get to it. Experiment with different brands to see which one your keet enjoys the best. It could easily be that your parakeet hates a plain tasting one but adores a banana tasting one.

Part of your role as a parakeet owner is to ensure your parakeet has access to all the vitamins and nutrients she needs to thrive. Minerals are definitely a part of this.

If the poop eating continues after your parakeet has been supplied with a full range of other mineral options, it is time to take her in to a vet for a check-up, to see what else might be amiss with your little pet.

Grit, Gravel and your Parakeet

What is Grit?

Grit is literally small pieces of gravel or rock. The use of grit and birds all began when scientists watched pigeons eat, and noticed that the pigeons ate their seeds, then ate some little rocks. They discovered that the rocks 'rolled around' in the pigeons' stomachs and helped to mash the food. They decided that *all* birds must need to eat rocks to digest their food, and soon people were buying grit to give to their parakeets, or putting gravel floor-paper in their parakeets' cages.

Do Parakeets Need Grit?

There has been over the years a pretty large debate over whether parakeets need grit / gravel in their diet. Every vet I have talked to in the last three years about this agrees completely that grit is *not* necessary for parakeets.

There *are* some birds such as pigeons that do need gravel. These birds eat seeds *whole* and the gravel helps their stomachs wear through that outer layer of seed to get to the inner nutritious part. Remembers, birds don't have teeth :). However, parakeets eat *soft* food and hull their seeds. So they only swallow the soft, inner parts of the seeds. They do *not* need gravel.

You might say, what's the harm? So what if they eat some rocks along with their food? Well imagine if *you* ate rocks. You have tender stomach lining that doesn't enjoy pointy stone things poking at it. The same is true for parakeets. In many cases gravel can cause harm to their digestive systems.

Not only that, but if you use gravel perches or gravel cage-bottoms, it rips up the feet of the parakeets, making them sore and perhaps even bleed. This is *not* a good idea. So keep all gravel and grit away from your budgie!

Cuttlebones

Think of your bird's beak like a long fingernail. It's made out of a tough material that's built to crack open seeds so the bird can eat the nutritious insides. The beak keeps growing, and the bird keeps wearing it down. Many times, though, the bird does not wear the beak down fast enough, and looks to find other ways to keep the beak the proper shape.

This is where the cuttlebone comes in. A cuttlebone can be found in most stores, and is simply a 'nail file' for birds. The birds naturally start gnawing on it when they want to trim their beaks. In the wild they would use all sorts of other natural items to do this sanding, but in a bird cage you have undoubtedly removed all of those nasty sorts of harsh materials. The bird isn't left with anything it can perform this important maintenance with.

If the beak really gets too long, where it starts to cut into the area below the bird's mouth, then it's time to take it to a vet to get a trim. This is a very rare situation, and usually only happens when there is no cuttlebone or other substance for the bird to do this naturally.

In addition to trimming a parakeet's beak, the cuttlebone is also full of calcium, just like other bones. Calcium is an important part of a parakeet's diet.

Note that female parakeets are naturally chewy birds. In their native Australian habitat, they would gnaw out holes in Eucalyptus trees to build their nests in. The female parakeet loves to gnaw. Be sure if you have a female that there are lots of things for her to gnaw on in her cage, from wooden toys to perches to cuttlebones.

Sometimes birds can be afraid of a cuttlebone when they first see it. Remember that for most birds, their cage is their "domain" and they don't like new scary things just appearing in it. So put the cuttlebone in the room but not in the cage for a few days, so they can get used to it. Then put it in the cage in a back corner, so they don't have to be near it until they get comfortable with it. If they're still afraid of it, try putting it on horizontally or cut it in half. Some birds are afraid of a big, vertical thing as it reminds them of big, overpowering birds.

Also, remember that keets have relatively small beaks. They aren't hinged like a snake's. If the cuttlebone is too big, they simply can't really use it. Make sure you get a small cuttlebone meant for a keet - not a gigantic one meant for a parrot.

What Is a Cuttlebone?

As the 'bone' part might indicate, the cuttlebone is the bone in a cuttlefish :). The cuttlefish is *Sepia officialis* - a mollusk. They are about 2' long and are built of a main body / head plus 10 tentacles. Most mollusks have shells outside their body, like oysters and

Mineral Block Information

In addition to cuttlebones, there are also mineral blocks, which are in essence artificial cuttlebones. Sometimes they are flavored and colored to make them look more interesting. Cuttlebones have around 35% calcium in them, so you want your mineral block to be somewhere in that 25%-35% range.

Buying a Parakeet

A parakeet is just about the *perfect* pet for a first-time owner. They're very easy to take care of. They're very intelligent and can even learn how to talk. And they're inexpensive, going from between $20 to $50 depending on the type you wish to purchase.

The following pages will walk you through the steps involved in getting your very own parakeet to love and care for.

Hand Raised Parakeets vs Bin-o-Budgies

To start with, no matter how you end up getting your parakeet, be sure to buy your parakeet from a reputable dealer. You don't want a sick parakeet that will die a week after you bring it home.

A "bin of budgies" bird is the bird that you find in the average pet store in a cage with a bunch of other birds. That bird has learned that birds are its friends and that humans are scary. It will take you weeks if not months of slow, patient effort to teach the bird to think of you as its flockmate. Also, because it was raised with birds, it has learned to talk like a bird and it is difficult for it to "switch gears" and start to try communicating in "human speech" with a human.

On the other hand, if you instead buy a hand-raised parakeet, those keets tend to make the best pets. They already think of humans as their "flock" and will be the best at sitting on your finger, being friendly, and learning to talk. Those are usually the $50 ones. It can literally save you months of training and bonding time if you purchase a hand raised parakeet or budgie.

A hand raised parakeet was raised by humans, and thinks it *is* a human. It is used to humans, to sitting on their fingers, to cuddling with them. Humans are its friends. It is used to human speech, and thinks that human speech is the normal way to communicate, So it is much more likely to begin talking at an early age and to learn a larger vocabulary.

In short, it is much better to buy a hand raised parakeet if you can! Yes, they cost a bit more money. But you're not just paying for "a fancy name." You are paying for hours and hours of time and energy that the breeder put into feeding, interacting with, and taking care of this bird. In return, you get a pet who is instantly cuddly and snuggly!

If you can only afford a $20 keet from a "bin-o-budgies" at the local store, just know that you'll have a much longer training time. You'll need to be patient, diligent, and caring. Your keet will come around and learn to adore you!

Choosing your Parakeet

When you choose a parakeet, find one that is friendly and alert. Don't go for the sleepy one that sits in the bottom of the cage. Go for the active one that rings the bells in the cage or looks at you with interest. Its wings might be clipped, but it should be able to hop around actively and maybe flutter from perch to perch.

You also want a very young one so that it is still quite impressionable. Look at the area right above the bird's nose. You want lots of stripes there. The fewer stripes, the older the bird is.

Look at this picture of my darling keet Nazo when she was a baby. Her entire front of her head is striped:

Now look at this photo of Santo and Pinto when

they are much older. See how the front of their heads are just white?

Before you bring your budgie home, make sure you have all of the necessary items ready. You don't want your budgie to have to sit in its take-home box for hours and hours while you work on getting the cage and everything else set up. So before you take the trip to buy the budgie, first make a trip to get the supplies.

What Color Keet should I Get?

Parakeets come in many different colors. In my years of owning keets I've had green parakeets, blue parakeets, spotted parakeets (for example blue and white), pale blue parakeets, and so on.

Parakeets come in yellow, purple, and other color variations!

Green is the "natural" color for a parakeet, and blue is another very popular color that has been bred. All of these are still parakeets, just like both a Great Dane and a Sheepdog are still dogs. They just look a bit different.

You can get any color the pet store has for you, and it will make no difference at all to the keet's personality. It's like you coloring your hair black or red. You are still you, it's just an external difference that you are making.

Some stores charge more for some colors. They do that because people will pay more :). It doesn't mean the keet is any different as far as "being a keet."

Should I Get One Keet or Two?

Parakeets are flock creatures. They love to live in groups. That being said, YOU can of course be a part of the parakeet's "group". It all comes down to how much time you spend at home with your parakeet.

Let's say you're a stay at home elderly person who is in the living room 99% of wakeful hours. Your keet sleeps at night when you do, so it doesn't matter where you are when the keet is asleep :) If you are always in the room with the keet, the keet will be completely happy having you as a companion. There's no need for another bird.

However, if you are away at school all day long, and only get home at 6pm just before your keet is falling asleep, then your keet is going to be alone all day. That is really cruel to do to a parakeet. Parakeets are meant to live in giant flocks, wheeling around in the sky. They consider being alone to be a very dangerous thing and in the wild they would do everything in their power to get back to the safety of the flock.

If you want to teach your keet to talk, then it is fine to have the keet alone for its first six months or so, while you work on that. Once that time is past, then it's really wise to get a second bird if you're not going to be around a lot.

Note that you should never get two birds of opposite genders unless you have talked to a vet, gotten books on breeding, and bought the equipment and medical supplies necessary. Breeding is a serious hobby to get into, and you need to be prepared beforehand.

What Sex Keet Should I Get?

Parakeets, like most creatures in the world, come in two sex types - male and female. The females are the ones that lay the eggs and keep the nests clean. The males are the ones that impregnate the females and protect their territory.

This means that in general the males are very vocal, and more easily learn how to talk and sing. In general the males are very "chewy" - they love to gnaw on things because they are practicing their valuable skill of hollowing out tree holes for nests.

That being said, it is nearly impossible to know for sure if a keet is male or female when it is young enough to buy and train. If you get a very old keet that is clearly male or female, it's past the training age where it's easy to train the bird. In fact, many people have old keets and still don't know whether they are male or female! The only way to know 100% for sure is to have a vet tell you. Anything else - guessing at nose color or personality - is pure guesswork.

Also, I know many male keets that gnaw and many female keets that talk and sing beautifully. Keets are all very unique creatures. I know keets that are shy, keets that are outgoing, keets that love carrots, keets that hate carrots, you name it. Every single keet you see in a store is going to be different, based on their own little brains. Just like you are different from other people in the world, because you have a special brain of your own.

In short, I wouldn't try to buy a bird based on gender. I would buy a bird that seemed the most lively, inquisitive, alert bird in the flock - that is also the youngest. That is the most important thing to look for.

First Keet Vet Visit

Any pet that you buy - whether it's a cat, a dog, a parrot or a parakeet - needs to be taken to a vet for an initial checkup. This checkup will tell you if there are any serious problems with the animal. Most pet stores and breeders offer you a 30 day guarantee on your pet's health. In this time, you need to have your pet checked out for serious medical issues. This is important for many reasons. Many illnesses if caught early can be fixed for little money - but if left to fester can cost you thousands in medical bills or put your pet through agonizing pain.

Also if something is seriously wrong with your pet, you will want to know both to alert the pet shop and so you can possibly return the pet or quarantine it and/or your family. It is really best to learn these things QUICKLY so they can be dealt with.

Be sure to factor in the cost of that vet visit to your

"start up costs" for your pet, along with the costs of the cage, food, and other basic supplies.

Some people do take their parakeets in for yearly checkups, just as you would take a dog or cat in. This helps ensure the pet's health. Other people find that the initial checkup is quite adequate, and that once they know they have a healthy pet, there is little need to keep taking the pet in.

You definitely want to establish that initial contact so your vet has your pet on record and will know who the pet is if you have a midnight emergency. But after that, you might be fine only taking the pet in if something seems seriously wrong with your pet's health.

Caring for your Parakeet

Now you have a nice, big cage, with fresh food and fresh water in it, some newspapers lining the bottom of it, and a nervous but alert little feathered creature within. What do you do now?

Well first, think of your first day of school. Wasn't it scary? You didn't know any- body and didn't know what you should do. It's just like that for this little bird. It's afraid, everything is new, and it doesn't have anywhere "safe" to run.

So let it learn that its cage is safe. Put the cage in the room you're in most of the time - not off in a corner somewhere that people only go when they sleep. If you're always in the kitchen, put the cage in the kitchen. If you're always in the computer room, put it in the computer room. But put it in a corner of the room where it can both see and hear everything, and also have a 'nook' that feels safe. Drape a cloth over the wall-side of the cage to give it even more safety.

Birds like to be 'up high' to be safe from cats and predators, so now your bird can sit high in the cage and have the cloth around it on a few sides. That is very safe feeling. It also keeps out drafts for when the bird sleeps.

Keep loud noises down. Talk normally, so the bird isn't afraid of the silence. Birds get very paranoid when it's completely silent, because this normally means (in the wild) that some sort of predator is around. So play soft music, talk quietly amongst your-selves and keep an eye on the bird. Eventually he'll realize that he's not going to be eaten. He'll start examining his cage, maybe taking a bite of food or a sip of water. He'll explore his new little world and see that really, it's not that bad. It's actually kind of nice.

Once your parakeet has gotten over the initial fright, keep him reminded that you are a part of his new world. Don't run to the cage, don't make loud noises. But wander over and talk sweetly to him. Tell him he's a good bird, a pretty bird. Parakeets love words with 'hard' sounds in them like K and B and T. They learn those words very quickly. If your parakeet was hand raised, he may already be ready for finger-sitting, but if you got a bin-o-budgies bird, it may take a while. So spend the next two weeks focusing on this, because this is key.

Once your bird is finger-trained, you can let him out to explore his new world! Make sure *all* doors are closed and it's even good to make a special sign to hang on each door saying DO NOT OPEN. You want to make sure it's extremely clear that a bird is loose so that the door stays shut. Birds love to fly! And now that your bird knows his home is the "safe place to return to" and also that your finger is the place to fly to, you can know that his explorations of the room will end with him returning home again.

Safety Checklist and Supplies

Parakeets are highly inquisitive creatures and are as smart as a 2 or 3 year old baby. They can get into *really* tiny corners and wedge themselves into holes when they are exploring. Be sure to never let a budgie roam around without you being there to help keep an eye on it. A parakeet is just like a human baby. They love to nibble at everything and try to get where they should not be. It's your role, as the "parent", to parakeet-proof your home and not keep any dangerous items around. You can never count on your para- keet to simply "avoid" the dangerous locations.

Very Important: Never bring a bird out when someone is cooking, period. Hundreds of birds are scalded because the owners figured "Oh the bird will never come into the kitchen." This danger has nothing to do with the bird's wings being clipped or unclipped. Clipped birds are just as likely (if not more) to fall into danger in the kitchen.

Explore each room in your home. Look for potential dangers in each one. Try to keep the house reasonably neat so a parakeet can't get lost or trapped under a pile of junk. Close the doors to any rooms which are simply too dangerous to try to fix, and make up door-hangers to put on them whenever the parakeet is out, that say "Parakeet is Loose - Keep Closed."

Parakeets

Always leave toilet seats down. Always. It'll be that one time you forget that the parakeet decides to race in there for fun. Don't leave other 'standing water' out like for cleaning the floor.

Food can be exceptionally dangerous for parakeets. They love to nibble. Make sure nothing harmful to eat is around. Don't leave out chocolate, even at holiday times! Don't allow any poisonous plants in the house at any time. Don't use anything poisonous that could get into the air - definitely no smoking, no cooking with Teflon, Do not use a self-cleaning oven cycle unless the windows are wide open and the birds are somewhere safe. No mite sprays, etc.

Don't forget to examine your walls and ceilings - birds can get just about anywhere. Don't use ceiling fans unless they are very slow. Many parakeets have been harmed or killed by spinning fan blades. Be sure to keep screens on all of your windows so the parakeet can't escape out a window.

Remember, it is your responsibility as the owner to keep the environment safe, not the bird's to know what to do and not to do. Think of it as having a crawling infant. Do you let an infant play upstairs and just say, "Now remember, don't go towards the stairs!" Or do you leash the child in one room? No, you gate the stairs so it is safe no matter what else happens, and you are always present with the child to watch it, just in case. Just as with an infant, do not let your parakeet out unattended. They are very curious and can easily crawl into some nook or cranny where they get stuck.

Why Parakeets Should Not be Left Home Alone and Loose

A few parakeet owners I know won't let even their keets out of the cage with unclipped wings, never mind the incredible thought of the human then walking out of the room ... out of the house ... and driving away while their parakeet was running around loose in a room. I have to convince them it's safe to leave the keet's wings unclipped, never mind take further risks. But it seems that a few parakeet owners out there feel it's fine to walk away from their house while their keet was free flying in a room.

NO.

A parakeet has the intelligence of a three-year-old toddler. If a parent drove off and left their 3 year old toddler roaming around a house without anyone there, they would be arrested for child abuse and the child would be sent to a better home. So you have to ask yourself, why is that? What could happen to this three-year-old toddler, let's say that the kid is sitting and watching TV in a room with the doors closed, while the parent is off drinking at the local bar for five or six hours?

Natural Events

OK, the obvious stuff first. Tons of kids, and parakeets, have died over the years in fires. If the pet is in a cage, the firefighters have a chance of grabbing the cage and rescuing it. I know keets that have been rescued like that. If the keet is flying loose around in the room, the firefighters have no chance. The keet often collapses to the floor from smoke inhalation. It burns alive. If the keet manages to fly out through a burned-out hole, the bird will then die of exposure.

Fire is not the only danger that strikes residences. There are trees that fall onto houses in high winds. There are cars that go off the road and plow into houses. There are sinkholes that open up and swallow houses whole. Earthquakes, tornadoes, hurricanes. Think it'll never happen to you? That's exactly what the other keet owners who wrote me thought, too.

Burglars

If you are there with your keet, you can control what happens. If you are NOT there, you have no control. Burglars break into homes. There were about 2.1 million burglaries in the US in 2002. That is a HUGE number. Just about every adult I know has had at least one burglary attempt happen in their life. In a house I lived in a number of years ago, a group of teens attempted to break into it while I was in it with my child. I scared them off. Nowadays I work from home, and just a short while ago someone tried to break into the house next to me while I was home. I saw the teen get out of the car and walk towards their house; I thought it was just a visitor. It was only the next day when we talked to our neighbor that we heard what had happened. If the burglars steal your stuff it's bad enough - but I doubt they'll think to keep the doors closed to keep your keet safe. Your keet could easily escape and suffer a long, lingering death.

Don't think it's only "bad neighborhoods" that have burglaries. Burglaries happen in every single town in the US. If you have a lock on your door, the burglars assume something in there is worth stealing.

Service Men

The gas can spring a leak and the gasman needs to come in to fix something. The electrical system can go haywire and need to be fixed. The plumber can come to fix the sink :). You are now going to trust that your keet *never* gets out of the room during this, while you're not there? Your keet's health is not something to take so lightly that you assume things will be OK without you there. It is your responsibility to ensure your keet IS safe and healthy. Your keet can't do that on his own! Your keet is only thinking at a 3 yr old's level. You are the parent, you are the responsible one who is the only one who can make these safety decisions. Either you make the right ones, or your keet can die. That is the serious and awesome responsibility you accepted when you agreed to be the owner of this living creature.

It just takes one cable TV repairman to open the wrong door while looking for the bathroom to cause your keet to panic, fly out of the room you had locked it in, and get to a deadly situation. The only thing you can guarantee if you are not there is that you cannot ensure your keet's safety. It is you responsibility to do so before you leave.

Hazards In the Room

Your bird doesn't have to get out of the room to have an issue. The purpose of a cage is to keep your keet in a reasonably confined area where they cannot fall far or build up enough momentum to cause themselves harm. Let's say something spooks your bird - thunder, lightning, a car engine outside. Your bird spooks and flies head-first into a wall, window, or mirror. Now your bird has a life threatening injury, maybe a broken wing and flowing blood - and there is nobody there to rush her to a hospital. Birds only have a tiny amount of blood in them. If the injury is not handled immediately, the bird will be dead before anyone even knows about it.

Birds love to gnaw and chew. Unless you live in an Amish settlement, you have electrical outlets and cables in your room. Your keet only needs to decide to give a nibble to your clock radio cord, and ZAP, her light will go out forever. You can say "but my keet has never chewed on wires before". That's exactly what other crying keet owners have told me, too.

Be a Responsible Parent

The aim of this article is not to scare you. It is to make you think. When parents come home with a newborn baby, they scour the house thoroughly from top to bottom for dangers. That is what the

'Household Safety Checklist' is about - it is about the house being safe while you watch over your pet. Even with a safe house, when a six-month-old is crawling around the floor, parents don't wave goodbye and take off to work for eight hours, leaving the baby roaming alone! The baby is always watched by someone.

You responsibility to your parakeet is just as solemn an obligation as a parent's obligation to a child. You cannot do things "because the keet made me" any more than a parent gives a child candy for breakfast, lunch and dinner just because the child screams. What about car seats? Even if a child screams, it must be put into a car seat while in a car, for its own safety. To fail in this task because "the child didn't want it" has led to many deaths. Death cannot be undone, it is a permanent mistake.

Being a parent isn't easy. But it is an awesome responsibility which you now possess. If you intend to stay the parent of your keet, then it is important that you fully accept all of the charges which that entails.

Emergency Supply Kit

Parakeets are just like human toddlers. They are incredibly inquisitive, and love to explore every nook and cranny they can get to. They love to hang upside down by their claws, and can fit into very small areas. This means that your keet might end up in a rough situation, even if you watch your keet every second he or she is out of the cage. Some keets can get injured in their cages, because their feet get caught in a toy or other such injuries.

It's important that you are ready for such a situation *before* it happens, rather than trying to hop in your car and go driving for supplies while your keet is injured. Find a plastic box to hold the supplies and keep them by the keet cage. That way if something happens, you can easily grab the box and start handling the situation.

Vet Phone Number

You don't want to be flipping through a phone book if you have a parakeet emergency. Parakeets are very tiny and only have a small amount of blood in them. Tape the phone number of your vet, and a backup number to another vet, on the front of your box. You want to call that vet immediately if something happens, to get advice on what to do.

Styptic Pencil

A styptic pencil is used by people who shave, to stop the bleeding. It is a coagulant that causes the blood to clot. This can help you buy some time for your keet, by stopping the bleeding until you can get him or her to help.

Mist Sprayer with Water

They sell tiny plastic mist sprayers, used for spraying plants. They are very cheap (50 cents or so) but are perfect for medical emergencies. This can spray off an injured area so you can get the styptic pencil to the actual wound and get it to stop bleeding.

Small, Soft Washcloth

An injured parakeet is going to be very scared and will probably bite in panic. Use a small, soft washcloth to gently take a hold of your keet, to examine the keet for injuries. If the keet is really in bad shape, use the utmost in care in moving her. You don't want to make things worse. With humans, they use a 'body board' to keep the body as straight as possible when they move it. With a keet, you can use a piece of cardboard if the keet is really injured. But most of the time it's a twisted foot or broken wing, and gently lifting the keet with a washcloth is more gentle.

Small Cage

Most keets come home from the pet store in a small cardboard box. Keep this, or another small cage, around if you're able to. If you need to take your keet to a vet, it's safest to do that in a small container that doesn't have any moving perches or swings or other items. You don't want anything to bump into your keet while you bring her to get looked at.

Millet

Yes, this is a treat - but it's a great distraction tool. If your keet is busy munching on millet, she might not mind that you are doing something mysterious to her foot.

NOTE: I AM NOT A VET! If you have ANY concern about your parakeet's health and safety, no 'far off person' on the web will be able to accurately diagnose the issue. You need to bring your keet to a real, live vet to see the symptoms first hand and take appropriate action.

Candles to Avoid

Candles have been used since the dawn of mankind. Until modern times, candles were very smoky and would stain the insides of homes with their black soot. Parakeets have very tiny bodies, and their lungs very easily fill up with smoke and soot. Think of the "canary in a coal mine". The reason they would bring in a canary is that the canary would die right away when a bad gas was in the air. They knew, then, that it was not safe for miners. You don't want your parakeet to do the same thing!

A key to a candle burning "cleanly" without smoke was trimming the wick. Until the 1800s, if you didn't trim the wick (i.e. regularly cut off the long used part) it would smoke and flicker. Modern candles have self-trimming wicks for the most part - but they still burn more clearly if you keep the wick trimmed. Any time you light a candle, make sure there is only a short 1/2" or less wick there to start with. Keep it trimmed properly to avoid smoke being set loose in the air.

There are several materials that candles can be made out of. Some common ones are beeswax (made from bee wax), soy (made from the soy bean), paraffin (hydrocarbon mix like kerosene) and tallow (animal fat). In medieval times it was the bees wax in high demand, because it burned extremely cleanly. Unfortunately it was also expensive.

A candle burns the cleanest if it's a taper style, or a votive - so that the excess wax drips down and doesn't create a pool. Candles that are "trapped" in a jar or container burn far less cleanly.

Beeswax is generally the cleanest burning wax there is - however by far the worst soot creator is scents and colors. Adding a scent or color to any wax type will make it a huge soot generator compared even to "stepping down" to a lower quality material. If you have keets in the room make sure you are only burning scentless, colorless candles. Also, as always, never leave a candle burning unattended. It only takes a few minutes for a knocked over candle to start a fire that could jeopardize the lives of the parakeets.

Candles and Odor

I wanted to comment on the thought that a candle burning *without* any scent removes odors. The theory behind this is that tiny odor particles in the air meet up with the flame and are turned into carbon (i.e. burned).

Remember when you smell something, it is that your nose sensors are interacting with tiny little chunks of floating matter. That is how smell works. So if a fish is cooking for example, part of the cooking process is that tiny bits of fish are lifted up by the steam and float around the room. Some float into your nose and you smell them. If those tiny bits float into the candle flame, they are turned into carbon and now the room is less smelly.

The problem is that, of course, a candle only has a tiny little flame and it really can't affect a whole room. The percentage of the little odor chunks that meet up with the flame to burn up is small. Other than that one action, a scentless candle doesn't "do anything". Where a scented candle makes tons of tiny little "good scent" chunks that float around, which is how it works.

Hopefully all those "good scent" chunks outnumber the "bad scent" chunks.

So that all being said it is far more effective to directly remove whatever is creating the odor scent chunks in the first place - i.e. clean the cage, replace the cage liner :). It's also safer too!

Training your Parakeet

Parakeets are *extremely* smart and friendly. It always breaks my heart to see a parakeet stuffed into a cage, never let out, never interacted with. Parakeets are flock birds! They thrive on being cuddled, being nuzzled, having that physical interaction with their flock. And if there is only one parakeet in the cage, that flock is you! Hand training is a critical part of owning and raising a happy parakeet.

If you have already bought your new parakeet and gotten the parakeet used to your home, it's time to now start hand-training it. You can't let a parakeet out to fly around the room until it understands that your hand is safe, and that your finger is a perch it should hop onto when you say "UP." So you need to work on this next.

If your parakeet was hand-raised, this is probably easy. Your parakeet probably already knows the command "up". Simply put your hand *slowly* into the cage, talking nicely to it. Then gently press your finger against its chest and say "UP" in a gentle but firm voice. She should step up onto your finger. Keep it still and say things like "good bird" in a soft, soothing voice. If your parakeet does this easily, then you're already ready for it to come out and enjoy a bit of flying around.

However, let's say you had to buy your keet from a Bin O Budgies and it is very skittish. You have to train it that you are a friend and to be trusted. Follow the step by step instructions below, and in a few weeks you will have a parakeet that will be your loving companion for years and years. DO NOT SKIP A STEP. Be sure to fully be complete with a step before moving on to the next. This is very important in having this training work properly!

Here's the summary. Each step will be gone into in detail in the coming pages.

STEP ONE - TRUSTING THE HAND

you simply get your parakeet used to your hand being in the cage.

STEP TWO - PERCH TRAINING

you train your parakeet to step up onto a perch on command.

STEP THREE - FINGER-PERCH TRAINING

you show your parakeet that it's OK to step on a perch that also has a finger attached to it.

STEP FOUR - FINGER TRAINING

still staying just in the cage, your parakeet learns that your finger is a safe perch to sit on.

STEP FIVE - OUT-OF-CAGE FINGER TRAINING

the parakeet learns that her trusted finger is safe to sit on, even if it's outside the cage.

The more you interact with your parakeet, the friendlier he will get! Soon you'll find he loves hanging out on your shoulder while you do things, nibbling on earrings or necklaces. When I work at my computer, my parakeets hang out on the curtain rod right next to me, chirping down at me.

Remember, none of this will happen instantly. If you bought a hand raised parakeet it might all happen on the first day - but people who buy budgies out of large bins are in essence buying wild birds. It can easily take several weeks to get your budgie used to you as a trusted person. You have to be patient and work on this every day, to let your parakeet learn about you and learn to trust you. It can't be rushed. Parakeets are extremely intelligent and need to learn to trust you on their own time.

Parakeets do NOT BITE unless they are being threatened. So as long as you are quiet and gentle and friendly with your parakeet, you will have a quite loving companion! In this photo Bob is pretending that Nazo is an Evil Vampire Nazo, but believe me, Nazo would never hurt a fly :)

Watch especially for when your parakeet is getting in new feathers - their bodies and heads are VERY itchy around now! They will LOVE it if you gently scratch at their heads for them, or nuzzle them underneath their beaks :).

Trusting the Hand

The most important thing for any parakeet to do is to TRUST you, that you will not hurt her. Nothing else can happen if the parakeet does not trust you, if she flies around like a maniac when you get near her cage.

So start your training simply with your hand. Your hand goes into the cage every single day to change the food and water. Do this very slowly and calmly, talking to your parakeet in a soft voice. Put on soothing music when it is time for you to put your hand in the cage.

Parakeets fluff up when they are content

You need to train your parakeet to think of your hand as a nice thing that brings fresh food, not a scary thing. Sometimes, put millet into the cage with this "Friendly Hand." Parakeets love millet!

Yes, your parakeet will fly away the first few days! But if you keep this up with gentle words and quiet movements, after a week or so the parakeet should be stationary while you change the food, even if stationary means hiding at the far corner of the cage. Your aim here is for your parakeet to be watching your hand, not to be flapping around like an insane creature.

Perch Training

Your parakeet *must* be used to your hand being in the cage before you start step two. If your parakeet still flies around when you put your hand in the cage, go back to step one - building the trust.

OK, so your parakeet watches your hand when you change the food and water now.

On the day you choose to start this step, play some soft music in the background, and have the room the parakeet is in quiet and restful. Change her food and water as you normally would, with her watching you. Now, after you do the food/water, pause for a moment. Quietly use your hand to take a short perch from their cage, preferably one on the opposite site of the cage as the bird is. Now your hand is in the cage and you are holding the perch loose. The perch you choose should be small enough that you can move it around the cage without hitting things (especially the parakeet!!)

Your budgie already knows that perches are for sitting on. She is not afraid of a perch! So hold the perch at ... "perch level" - that is, at the same level as the perch your keet is currently sitting on. That is non-threatening to the bird.

Now move the perch *slowly* towards your parakeet, talking quietly to her. She'll be nervous to see a perch moving, but so far she should trust you, your hand, and the perch. There is no "new" or "scary" thing in her world.

When the perch nears her feet, raise it up a little bit so it is at the level of her legs. If she flies away at this point, stay still for a little while, and then start quietly moving the perch again, talking quietly to her. If she flies away four times in a row, tell her she's a good girl for trying and come back to it tomorrow. It should only take a day or two before she's used to the 'moving perch' and does not mind that it gets close to her.

When she is at this point, press the perch gently against her legs / lower chest. Say "UP" in a firm voice (not loud, just encouraging and firm) as you gently press. She will start to lose her balance backwards and naturally put her foot forwards, onto the new perch, for balance.

Note again that this probably won't happen on the first time! Your parakeet may sit there afraid, not willing to step on the perch. Your keet may just put one foot onto it but not be willing to "commit" both feet. Again, this is a training process. Keep trying each day until your bird learns this is not scary and is willing to put both feet onto the perch.

When your keet does step fully onto the new perch you are holding, hold it very steady! Your parakeet is trusting you with her life, you literally have her in your hands. Praise the bird enthusiastically and tell her what a good bird she is. After a short while, move the perch towards another perch in the cage so she gets off the one you're holding.

After she gets used to the perch, you'll find she hops onto the perch pretty easily when she sees it coming towards her. Then it's time to move to the next step.

Finger-Perch Training

Before you can finger-perch train your parakeet, your parakeet *must* be comfortable getting "up" onto a moving perch that you push against her. Be sure to finish perch training your parakeet before you move on to this step.

So now your parakeet knows that a perch in your hand is a trustworthy thing to sit on. She readily gets onto a perch that you move against her. She is learning to trust you as a "thing to sit on."

When you are ready to begin this step, prepare the room as usual - have it quiet, soft music playing. Change the food and water as usual. Remove one of the smaller perches from the cage. This time, however, put your finger on top of the perch. That is, hold the perch in your hand and stretch your second finger out (the one you point with) so it lays on top of the perch. Now the "perch" is a thick perch made up of the wood/plastic below and your finger above.

Once again, move this perch slowly towards your parakeet. Your parakeet is by now used to this and doesn't really think much of the fact that the perch has an extra bit of thickness to it. When you say UP to your keet, she should step onto the "perch", which is now your finger and the wood/plastic. Maybe the keet is on the perch part, maybe she's on the finger part, maybe she's half and half. Either way is OK.

Stay very still and praise her! She has gotten onto the offered perch without a problem. If she balks, go

back to just the perch until she is comfortable with
that, and then try again.

Do this exercise a few times a day for a few days
until she learns that the finger- perch is a quite
reasonable place to sit. If she keeps sitting on the perch
part and not your finger part, try finding a shorter
perch so that the perch length IS your finger length and
she doesn't really have a choice.

Finger Training

At this point your parakeet should be quite comfortable sitting on a perch made up of the base perch (wood/plastic) and your finger. If your parakeet is not at that stage yet, go Finger-Perch Train your Parakeet.

You can probably guess what the next step is here. Go through your normal morning routine - soft music, quiet room. Change the food and water. This time do NOT take the perch from the side of the cage. Just move your hand over TO that perch and slowly stick your finger out over the perch.

Slowly move your hand with the stuck-out finger towards your parakeet. Your keet should be very comfortable with a moving hand and a sticking-out perch like thing at this point and not think anything of it. Press your finger softly against the leg / lower chest area of your parakeet, saying "UP" quietly but firmly. Your parakeet should step up onto your finger!

Note that parakeets LIKE sitting on fingers, from a sensory point of view. They have soft little feet! Wood and plastic is hard on them, and it's not like they can wear socks or lie down. The have to be sitting on their feet ALL DAY and ALL NIGHT. Your nice, soft finger is like a heavenly bed to them! It's warm, gentle on the tender feet, soft, just what every parakeet would dream about sitting on.

Praise your parakeet for sitting on your finger. Don't move your hand around! Let your keet get used to sitting on the finger, just relaxing there. Some parakeets will even fall asleep on the finger because it's so comfortable. When you are done, move your finger slowly to another perch so she can hop off.

This is a CRITICAL step in finger training, so spend a lot of time on it. Your para- keet needs to learn that your finger is a safe spot, a DESIRED spot to sit on. Any time your parakeet gets out of the cage, you need to be able to get her back IN her cage in case of emergency. So she needs to promptly get onto your finger if you ask her to, so you can move her to safety.

Out of Cage Finger Training

You MUST have your parakeet hand trained before you can bring her out of the cage. There are SO many emergency situations that can arise that require you getting your keet into its cage quickly for safety. A fire could break out, someone could put a Teflon pan on the stove, someone could open the doors so there is a clear path to the outside world. You need to get your parakeet on your hand and into the cage. Be sure to Finger Train Your Parakeet before attempting this next step.

Once your parakeet is fully finger / hand trained, it is time to consider letting her out of her cage. Parakeets are EXTREMELY intelligent creatures and if you leave her locked in her cage for her entire life, she will go stir crazy! She wants to explore at least the room she's in, climb around, fly if she can, look down at the room from the curtain rods. She'll enjoy a play-gym, or just hanging out on your shoulders.

So go through your morning routine. Quiet music, quiet talking. Seal ALL doors to this room though and put signs on them so people know not to come in.

When you're ready, move your hand towards your parakeet. Say "UP" and get your parakeet on your hand. Now SLOWLY bring the hand towards the opening in the cage. Your parakeet may be nervous! Up until now, your parakeet has thought of her cage as the location of safety and comfort. You're trying to bring her out of this safe area! It can really help to hold a stick of millet in your other hand, just by the cage door. Bring the parakeet just to the cage door area, not "out into the scary world". Let her sit there and eat millet. When she's done, put her back onto a perch.

The next day, bring her a bit further out, so she's at the entry-way to her cage. My parakeets love to sit on their "front porch" and just survey their world, even sleeping there. If you have a drawbridge-style entrance this is IDEAL, it can sit open and they can sit there or land there. If you don't have a drawbridge, it might be wise to make one by putting a rope perch or something else at the entry area (on the outside of the cage) so your keets have somewhere to sit.

If your keet starts flying or hopping around, don't panic. Let them settle down and explore. When they are quiet, you can always get them back onto your hand with "UP" and bring them back to the cage. If they can fly, they will fly back to their cage on their own when they are ready to take a nap. Their cage is their home.

Find ways to encourage your parakeet to enjoy

the room. Most parakeets love curtain-rod sitting. I'd advise putting some paper towels beneath the rods if you do this, their poops are easier to clean up that way. I put the parakeets' bathtubs on top of their cage - that way when they come out they can take their baths, and their bathtubs are always fresh and clean. I also have a parakeet play gym at the cage's side, so they can go back and forth from the play-gym to the cage as they wish.

Do NOT let your parakeets just roam around without you being there. Keets are very curious and can easily get themselves into trouble. They can wedge themselves behind bookcases or under couches. You need to be there and aware, so you can rescue them. You don't have to watch them every second - I work on my computer while they fly and hop around me. But I do check every ten minutes or so to make sure there are still three of them in sight :).

Lisa Shea

Interacting with your Parakeet

Many people who are new to parakeets have some very unusual ideas about how they are going to interact with their parakeets. Some think they will sleep with their keets. Some imagine taking them out for walks. Some think keets will be petted, like a cat or a dog.

It's important to remember first that you can do NOTHING outside of the cage with your keet until it is fully hand trained. I have complete step by step instructions on this site on how to hand train your keet. You have to work at it daily, to fully build the trust of the keet in you. Hand training isn't magical or mystical. It is solely about the keet learning to trust you as a person that he can rely on. It's not something you can "trick". Trust is something that is earned.

Once you have built up that bond of friendship and trust, your keet is NATURALLY going to want to be with you. It's the same as you and your best friend. It's not that your best friend "tricked" you. It's that you two spent time together, you learned to like each other, and now you voluntarily choose to spend time with each other. It's not that your mom says "you must go spend time with Billy" and you say "I don't want to!!" It's that you actively want to go play with Billy. The same is true with a keet who has learned to love you. The keet WANTS to be with you and actively flies to you to be near you.

This level of love and affection doesn't spring into being in a day or a week. You build it up over weeks and months. Remember, a parakeet can live to be 15 years or older! You will have years and years to spend with your keet.

How Will We Interact?

The reason that cats and dogs like to be petted is that, when they were babies, their parents licked them all over to keep them clean. Cats and dogs equate long, gentle strokes on their skin with "love". It's the same reason cats knead - they kneaded as kittens to turn on their mom's breasts. The reason they do these things as adults is it brings back fond memories of their childhood.

Parakeets are NOT licked all over by their mommy parakeets. They are in fact not touched at all. They are FED. That's the interaction they have with their parents. To a bird, touch is scary. Touch is what happens when an enemy is near and is about to eat them. Therefore, most parakeets simply don't like to be "petted". It's not a normal sensation they ever get in the wild.

There's two exceptions to this. The first is when a

keet is itchy, they rub against something to relieve the itch. Sometimes they will even convince a nearby other keet (assuming there are other keets around) to preen them in their itchy spot. So if you really build a strong connection with your keet, she might let you "itch" her under her chin or over her eyes. It will take a long time before she trusts you to this degree, so don't rush it. Some keets never feel comfortable with being itched. With Nazo, our green keet, she loved being scratched when she was a baby - but refuses to be touched now that she is an adult. Keets have very individual personalities and each one is different.

The second exception is that keets of course have sex to make baby keets. That involves touch. Once your keet reaches sexual maturity (say around 8 months old) he/she might be interested in sexual sort of contact with you, since your keet "loves" you. A male keet might try to push his sex organ into your hand to have a baby with you. A female keet might try to get underneath you, since a male parakeet will get on top of the female parakeet to have sex with her. It doesn't matter of course if YOU are male or female. The keet really doesn't understand human bodies that well. All your keet knows is that she loves you and wants to have babies with you, because that's what keets that are in love do.

Don't yell at your keet or be upset if he does this sort of thing. It's just natural for a keet to want to have babies. Tell your keet that you love him very much, and that it's just not possible for you two to create parakeet chicks :).

Do Not Train in the Bathroom

When you are doing your hand training sessions, it is always best to do those right in the room that has the cage - because you should not have your keet out of the cage if it is not yet trained. You should not move the cage for a session of training, because the entire point of training is that you are building trust in as relaxed, "normal" environment as possible. The moment you move the cage, they are going to be nervous - which goes against the purpose of training.

The bathroom, in particular, is one of the *worst* possible places to have an untrained keet. Why? Let's start with reason 1 - it is a room explicitly for humans to pee and poop. Remember that rule about never making parakeet toys from toilet tissue rolls, because the rolls are probably contaminated? The same is true for the counters, floors and other surfaces around a toilet. Toilets are not "hermetically sealed". When you use a toilet, particulates go into the air. That is especially true if you have males in the house. Any surface a keet touches could easily make that keet very sick.

How about if I really clean it? Well, let's think about the cleansers used in bathrooms. Some of them are so incredibly toxic that they tell *humans* to only use them with gloves and an open window. This is stuff that could kill a keet with a drop. Now, if you have scrubbed your bathroom floor, surfaces and counters with these toxic chemicals then it's clean - but it is deadly to small animals. That's the whole point of the cleansers, to kill living bacteria and germs.

Even beyond that, the very construction of a bathroom is keet unfriendly. The toilet is undoubtedly porcelain, which is an incredibly hard ceramic which can kill a falling keet on impact. The bathroom counter / sink area is probably porcelain as well, if it isn't marble (stone). The bathtub is probably porcelain too. The floor is probably tile. This room is full of hard surfaces that can seriously harm a fast moving keet.

Never mind the large mirror that pretty much every bathroom has over the sink - a sure way to cause a keet to fly head-first into the glass.

The number of email messages I have received from people who had their keets injured in their bathroom is pretty staggering. The only time a keet should *ever* be in a bathroom is when they are fully trained, with you, and using either the sink or shower to bathe. In both cases that area should be thoroughly cleaned with *water only* and perhaps baking soda, to remove every single trace of toothpaste, mouthwash, and other chemicals that might be there.

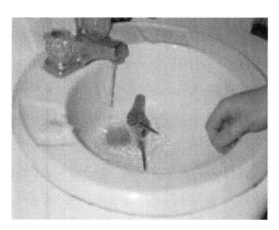

Biting Problems

Parakeets are relatively small creatures with very little in the way of defenses. They don't have stinky odors like a skunk, or razor-sharp claws like a tiger. All they have to defend themselves with is their beak. If they feel afraid, that is the only way they have to defend themselves. And since the original word for budgie in Australian aborigine means "good to eat", there are a lot of creatures a parakeet had to defend itself against!

Usually a parakeet that is biting is feeling afraid. And usually that's because you're jumping ahead in your interactions with the parakeet. You are the owner, you are the one "in charge" that has to get your pet used to his new surroundings. You have to first give him time to settle into his cage. You then have to move slowly through the hand training instructions, not going too fast. Make sure the parakeet is thoroughly accepting one stage before you move on to the next stage.

Most cages can be cleaned without putting your hands into the cage. Many modern cages even let you change the water and food without putting your fingers into the cage. Think of the cage as the parakeet's safe sanctuary. Let's say you were in your favorite treehouse, where you were safe. Now say a gigantic hand came reaching down for you from the sky. You'd try to defend yourself in your treehouse, right? That's all that the parakeet is doing. You have to teach him, slowly, patiently, to trust you. But it won't just happen in days, or even in weeks. Especially if you have an older keet or one from a bin-of-budgies, it might take months. But you will be developing a friendship that will endure for years and years.

Really, the essence of not being bit is to not put your fingers near a bird that is afraid. If your bird is not hand trained, your hand should not be near it. Talk quietly and soothingly to your bird. Keep the stress levels down, by not introducing new birds until the birds are thoroughly familiar with each other (in separate levels) and letting the bird have a full 8 hours of fully dark, quiet sleep each night. Just like humans, birds get cranky if they don't get enough sleep, or if they are harassed while they are awake.

If your bird does bite, NEVER hit it. That will only make your bird more afraid, scared, and feeling threatened. Don't use water sprays (like some people do on cats) - water needs to be a healthy, normal thing for your bird. Just say NO in a loud, firm voice, and put a blanket over the cage to hide him from his world. That will both help him calm down and make him feel lonely, which is the punishment birds enjoy the least.

Teaching a Parakeet to Talk

The key to teaching a parakeet to talk is to have the parakeet think it's part of the "human flock", and therefore that it needs to communicate with its human friends. If you have a mirror in the cage, or other parakeets, it will see parakeets around it and want to talk like them (i.e. chirp). So step one is to have your young parakeet on its own, surrounded by humans that talk to it.

The younger the better, as in all things that involve learning. Get a hand fed parakeet if you can, at a very young age. That is when it's still learning how to communicate, and talking "human" will be a valid option for it. While male parakeets tend to talk better than female parakeets do, both can certainly talk!

Birds learn best in the morning, when their mind is fresh and ready for new information. If you use a towel or cover over your bird's cage, talk to them for 1/2 hr before you remove it each morning. Repeat the same phrases loudly, slowly and clearly. Parakeets do best with hard letters like K and T, so the traditional "hello" is actually sort of hard for a Parakeet. "Cutie" would be much better! Parakeets tend to mumble and to talk quickly, so the more slowly you talk, the more normal it will sound when the bird starts to repeat it.

Have patience, and eventually your parakeet will start to answer back to you! Once they get the hang of it, they'll learn more and more quickly as you go. While you can try taping yourself and playing the tape, the parakeet really needs to learn that this is a way for you and it to talk to each other. So it works best if you physically talk to your para- keet, and that you do it often.

Parakeets can also learn to mimic other sounds around them. They can learn to chirp like a cell phone, whistle a short tune, and much more! I've taught my parakeets to sing like chickadees, which drives the chickadees outside the windows crazy :).

Parakeet Bodies

Parakeets are small animals with a simple system. They do not need large amounts of care to remain healthy, but they do require *some* care! The four main body areas that you need to keep an eye on are the parakeet's wings, claws, beak, and eyes.

These pages will provide a summary of the things you should understand, so you can do quick troubleshooting of your keet acting odd. Always be prepared to call a vet, though. Keets have tiny bodies and can go from "slightly sick" to "quite ill" in a short period of time.

Feathers – The Basics

Parakeets and budgies are birds, so naturally one of their primary descriptors is that they have feathers! When you first see a bird it's easy to think "Oh feathers are all alike". But it's amazing when you have your own pet bird in your home 24 hours a day how quickly you realize feathers are NOT all alike! It's like saying children are all alike. Sure they all have legs and arms, but if you spend time in a kindergarten class you find quickly that each little child has his or her own opinions, wants, desires and attitudes.

OK, this is Nazo, my green parakeet. Take a look at her picture. She has long flight feathers on her wings, which let her fly. Those are the feathers that most people think about. There are long feathers in her tail, which help her steer. But she ALSO has short, fluffy feathers on her chest, which help to keep her warm. She has even tinier feathers on her head, which are for decoration.

Above are some of the longer feathers. These fall out maybe twice a year, as new feathers grow in. They do not fall out all at once - if they did, she'd become unable to fly, and become a tasty treat for whatever predator was around! So the feathers fall out on a random schedule, so there are always enough feathers left to keep her aloft.

The above downy chest feathers seem to fall out ALL the time, being replaced with fresh, fluffy feathers. Parakeets shed the most in the spring and fall, as their bodies gear around to the new seasons. This is a good reason to keep a cage shield on the lower part of your parakeet cage, to keep these downy feathers from falling onto the ground. Not that they're really troublesome, but you end up with a bunch each week to vacuum up during those seasons. The parakeets pull some out during their normal preening and others fall out as they fly around during their exercise time. It's quite normal, just like you lose hair every time you brush your hair with a brush.

Next, look at Pinto. You can see how different all of the various feathers look on her. Not only are her head feathers different from her body feathers, but she even has different types of colors on various parts of her body.

In the below image, Santo has her wings fully stretched out as she lands on Bob's hand. You can see all of the flight feathers in her wings, and the "steering" feathers of her tail.

Parakeets

Clipping Parakeet Wings

I once had a parakeet owner write me saying, "Why don't you clip your parakeets' wings? It's too dangerous to let them fly." This question addresses the safety issue from completely the wrong end! Your primary task as the owner of a parakeet is to make their environment safe, not have to "restrict the bird" for its own good. Clipping a bird's wings is no substitute for substantive safety precautions.

No matter how well you clip a parakeet's wings, they can still get around their area. Many owners become laid back in their tending of the parakeet figuring it is "hobbled". But very quickly, parakeets learn how to use their shortened wings to glide, and as the wings grow out they are more and more able to get to new locations. You cannot plan for your parakeet NOT being able to get to locations. You have to make your entire home parakeet safe just in CASE your parakeet does indeed get somewhere it does not belong.

Read through the parakeet safety tips on how to keep your house parakeet safe. You have a very solemn responsibility, as owner of the parakeet, to keep it safe from harm. A parakeet is like an inquisitive three-year-old. You can't just tell the three-year-old "don't drink that purple liquid, it is deadly." You have to make sure the purple liquid is locked up and not available. In the same manner, you must make sure your home is free of poisons and dangerous surfaces that your parakeet might, however much by mistake, stumble onto.

Bob made this keet-safe play area

Parakeets are meant to roam hundreds of miles through an interesting variety of terrain in their native homelands of Australia. They get new sights, new sounds, new smells. Parakeets are extremely intelligent and will get bored quickly if you just confine them to one small cage in one room for years and years. Think of how much YOU would be unhappy if you were stuck in a cube for your entire life!

So once your home is safe, let them out to explore it. Play different music for them, give them new, healthy snacks to eat. Let them hang out with you while you watch TV or play the piano. Your parakeet will thank you for the experiences!

Bird Feathers and Wings

Parakeets have an average of 2,000 to 3,000 feathers on their bodies. The feathers are of several types. First, there are soft down feathers close to their body, that are fluffy and help keep them warm. Next are the contour feathers. These are the colored feathers around the body, as well as the small scalloped ones on the head that are normally white on the very outside, black in the middle and a color in the inside. These are for decoration and warmth. There are also small "semi-plume" feathers around the face.

Perhaps most importantly, parakeets have flight feathers that help it fly. These are the long feathers on each wing.

Parakeets do a good job of keeping their feathers

clean since the feathers are so important to their survival. They will preen, wash and fluff their feathers regularly. Be sure to give them clean bathwater daily so they can splash around and wash off any dirt or grit.

Birds molt during certain seasons, just like many cats, dogs and other creatures do. This helps them shed the 'warmth' feathers when it is hot out, for example. If you notice your bird has shed a lot of feathers in the late spring, or has dropped a number of feathers in the fall as the winter ones grow in, this is a normal part of the seasonal cycle.

If your parakeet is under a great deal of stress, you might notice strange white lines or even holes in the feathers on your bird. It would be important to talk with a vet to help find out what is stressing your bird, and maybe to give it special food to help it become healthy again. Also if you ever notice your bird holding its wing out or suddenly unable to fly where it could before, take it to a vet to look for the possibility of an injury.

Molting and New Feathers

Just like humans, parakeets grow new feathers pretty constantly. So it is normal to see feathers fall out occasionally as new ones grow in. They also go through seasonal molts, just like dogs and cats do. So when springtime comes around, it's normal for a keet to shed its old feathers and start growing in lots of fresh, new ones. Of course they don't go COMPLETELY featherless during this - just like a dog doesn't turn completely hairless. But they do lose more than normal for a week or two, and then the new ones come in.

Here is a photo of Nazo with new head feathers coming in -

Parakeets

You can see the little rolled up new feathers poking out of her head. They look like thin scrolls of rolled up paper. They will soon unroll and look like fresh, lovely feathers. Parakeets get VERY itchy during this phase and it's hard for them to scratch their own heads. They have no hands! So you might see your keet rubbing her head on the cage bars or even want you to scratch her head for her (if she is fully hand trained and trusts you).

If your keet KEEPS losing feathers over a long period of time, or actually loses enough feathers to show skin, call a vet.

Here's an image of Pinto who is moulting. Note that it LOOKS sort of icky, but really it isn't. The "bare spots" you see on her body are really just the way she's fluffed up, she has a normal layer of feathers. On her head, you can see the rolled up brand new feathers as they are growing in. Once a feather fully grows in, it unfurls and looks like a normal feather.

Here's a close-up for a better look at the feathers.

Preening

The most important part of a parakeet's body is its wings. In its native Australian grasslands, the wings allowed a parakeet to escape from predators and find food. The parakeet spends time every day caring for its wings, preening them and keeping them clean.

A parakeet loves to take a bath to keep its wings very clean. But even beyond bath-time, a parakeet will preen its wings, keeping them in good working order. This involves ruffling through the feathers with his beak, sliding the longer feathers through his beak, scratching at his head with his claws, and fluffing out his feathers to shake out any dust.

This next picture is of Pinto trying to preen her chest feathers. If you see a bird is really itchy, maybe because new feathers are growing in, you can often help out by nuzzling the itchy area of the bird with your finger. You'll find that *especially* when new head-feathers are growing in, your parakeet will love this!

Note that if a parakeet starts actually YANKING OUT feathers, this is a sign of stress. Your parakeet should not be deliberately pulling out feathers, either from his own body or from those of his flockmates. While feathers do naturally molt and get replaced automatically, if your parakeet is yanking out numerous feathers it's time to talk to a vet.

Claws and Feet

Parakeets have *zygodactyl* claws, meaning that two point forward and two point backwards. This helps a parakeet climb in all directions and cling onto vertical surfaces.

A parakeet's claws are just like your fingernails - they are made of a hard substance that can't feel pain. However, their soft, pink flesh IS sensitive. You should never put gravel on the bottom of the cage or on your perches. That will scrape open the parakeet's flesh and cause sores.

You should give your parakeet a variety of perch types to sit on - soft rope perches, various sizes of wooden perches, even natural wood twigs. That will let the parakeet exercise his or her feet and sit in comfort.

While your bird's claws should naturally stay trimmed as it does its normal climbing about, it might happen that your bird's claw gets to be too long. A claw nail is too long when it starts to wrap back in onto itself - instead of forming a letter C it starts to try to form a letter O. Of course this is bad for the bird because now the bird can't sit on a perch - the claw is not able to hold on.

Pet shops sell bird claw trimmers which are in essence like little scissors. Before you attempt a claw trimming, be sure to have a styptic pencil within easy reach so, if you do cause the bird to start bleeding, you can stop it immediately.

First, you need to get the bird into your hand. The easiest way for me to do this is to get the bird to sit on my finger and then to trap his feet with my thumb over his feet. Do it gently!

Now put a washcloth across the top of the bird's back and put the palm of your other hand on top of the washcloth. Form an O with your thumb and forefinger around the bird's neck, using the washcloth to protect your fingers from being ... nibbled on.

Turn your hand so the bird is now on its back, nestled in the washcloth, with your thumb and forefinger holding him in place GENTLY. The bird will be quite nervous of course but if you're calm and soothing about it he shouldn't go too wild.

Now use the other hand (or have a friend help) and trim just the TIPS of each claw nail. You never want to cut down to where you see the blood vessel in the nail. Trim just enough to get the nail back into a C shape. You want the bird to still be able to hold on to perches and the side of the cage. You just don't want the bird's nail to be so curved that it is no longer able to sit on perches or climb on the cage.

If you run into any trouble with the trimming

process, or if your parakeet starts refusing to put weight onto one of its feet, be sure to take him to a vet immediately. While birds do sleep with one foot up sometimes, it should not be a 24 hour a day thing.

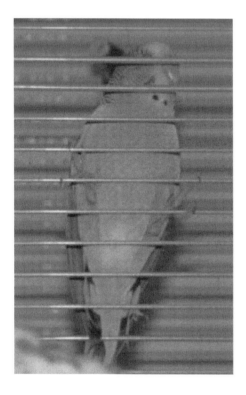

The Metal Band on a Keet's Leg

Many breeders put a metal band around one of a baby budgie's leg, when they are around 10 days old. The band itself costs about $8 each, although you can of course buy in bulk. The band typically tells the birth year of the budgie, as well as the breeder's ID number. As the budgie grows, the foot becomes more stiff and the band becomes unable to slide back off the foot.

Pros

The theory is that the band will help you identify a budgie that escapes. However, most escaped budgies aren't found again - and those that are tend to be easily identified by their owners. There aren't hundreds of budgies languishing in pet rescue facilities, that owners have not claimed.

Many parakeet shows require all entrants to be banded so they can be tracked. So if you have intentions of "showing" your bird in competition, you will need the bird to be banded. In fact, the American Budgerigar Society has colors assigned to each year to make it easy to see how old a budgie is. For example, older colors were:

2001 - Black
2002 - Yellow
2003 - Silver

Cons

A metal band permanently wrapped around your leg - a leg you stand on 24 hours a day - is not necessarily a comfortable thing. I hear from people often that have various issues with the band. Sometimes it gets caught on something, trapping the parakeet. It can cause a fractured leg if for example the band gets caught on a cage wire and then the bird falls as it tries to get itself untrapped.

The band itself is metal and can have small bumps in it that wear on the parakeet after a while. Sometimes the band presses against the foot or leg to cause swelling or uncomfortableness.

While some pet owners band expensive pets, like $1,000 parrots, there really aren't "parakeet thieves" out there targeting these little $20 pets. If there WAS a parakeet thief, he would simply cut off the band once he got his hands on the prized bird.

Band Removal

If you're going to have a band removed, have a vet who has done it before perform the task. There are many horror stories out there about permanently injuring a parakeet with a botched band removal job. In essence the vet will have to use tiny bolt cutters to get the band off.

Cere, Nose and Beak

The Cere of a parakeet is the "bump" above her beak - and is in essence her nose. There are two holes in it that she breathes through. The cere lets a parakeet breathe and smell.

When parakeets are babies the ceres are often just blue. As parakeets age the ceres usually mature to certain colors based on their sex. Female parakeets develop brown or pink ceres. Male parakeets develop blue ceres. Of course, there are many ceres that are in-between colors. The only real way to know the sex of a parakeet is to take it to your vet and ask!

The above picture is of Pinto, one of my three female parakeets. You can see her cere is pinkish.

This is all three of my female parakeets. Their ceres range from pink to brown. When a parakeet is young the cere is soft, but as they age it gets wrinkly and dry. That's fine, it's just what happens to keets.

Here's a user submitted photo of "Snow". Snow's cere is light blue, meaning he probably is a boy. You can never really be sure, though. A joke in the parakeet world is that you're only sure a parakeet is female when you see an egg come out of her :) And you can only tell a parakeet is male if he gets "excited" and you see his sex organ poking out of his feathers!

Lisa Shea

Eye Basic Anatomy

A parakeet should of course have two eyes, just like most other creatures. Having two eyes allows a parakeet to keep watch for predators very easily. Keets do not need super-sharp eyes to spot prey, like an owl or a hawk does. Parakeets don't tend to eat things that scurry away from them :) On the other hand, lots of creatures like to eat parakeets. Therefore, parakeets have to be able to spot danger quickly, and to escape from it.

Parakeets have eyes with two main parts - the inner black pupil, and the outer white part. This is similar to most other animals. Like you learned in biology class, the pupil lets the light in, so the animal can see. Parakeets can see in color, and have vision similar to but better than a human's.

Parakeets do have eyelids, which they can close when they sleep or when they want to brush dirt specks out of their eyes. They have little eyelashes on their eyelids to help keep their eyes clean.

Parakeets

Eye Changes As They Age

When parakeets are very young, their eyes are mostly pupil - i.e. they look solid black. Here's a photo of Nazo when she was a baby.

As parakeets mature, they get more and more white in their eyes. By 6 months or so, they have their adult eye configuration. It's not necessarily BRIGHT white on the edges. Here's an image of Ivory, and you can see that there is a ring of lighter color in her eye around the darker pupil.

So really, the only thing you can tell by looking at a parakeet's eyes is if they are "really young" or "not really young". Once they mature, you can't tell how old they are, i.e. that they're one year old or 10 years old.

How Well Can a Parakeet See?

Parakeets were not prey-eating animals. They didn't have to hunt down mice and rats. They mostly ate seeds, greens, small insects, other tiny items. Hearing and smell and taste really weren't high on the importance chart for parakeets. Parakeets have very low levels of hearing - they didn't need to hear mice scampering in the grasses to eat them. They didn't really taste buds - it didn't matter how yummy a stalk of millet was. But they DID need very good eyesight. When they were flying in giant flocks of 2,000 or 3,000 birds over an Australian plain, they needed to be able to spot that nice area of grasses with fresh seeds. Eyesight was critical to parakeets, for them to survive.

Parakeet eyesight is even more powerful than that of humans. Us humans have a variety of senses - we have a lot of tastebuds to see if something is sweet or sour, bitter or tart. But parakeets didn't go around eating rotten meat or other iffy substances. To them, taste wasn't that critical. It came down to sight. They had to see things, and they had to see FRESH things.

What is cool about a parakeet's eyesight is not only is it very sharp - but it is very useful. When we humans look at a parakeet's feathers, we just see blue or green or yellow. When a parakeet looks at another parakeet, they see into the ultraviolet spectrum. That is, they see if that parakeet has been out in a lot of sunlight recently. A parakeet's face feathers fluoresce when they are out in a lot of sunshine. That is a sign of a healthy keet. Keets can see that in each other's faces, in the fluorescence of the face feathers.

Keets can even tell if food is fresh. If you try to feed a keet old veggies, the keet will be very smart and refuse them. Keet's eyesight can see into spectrums to actually see if vegetables and fruits are fresh or old. This was of course of critical importance to a keet's survival. They mostly ate fruits and vegetables. If something was rotten, they wanted to know it BEFORE they ate it. It wasn't about smell or taste. It was about looking at it. They can look at a food item and know right there that it's fresh.

When you feed our keets fruits and veggies, give them the very freshest that you get! Then remove them after a few hours. Wilted lettuce and moldy carrots will not appeal to your keets!

Pinning - Dilated Eyes

When a keet gets excited about something, she will often make her eyes go really wide. Humans and other animals do this too. The pupil will become really small, so that in comparison the whites will really stand out.

This is a sign that your keet is excited about something - so it's important to figure out if that is a happy excitement ("Great! My favorite toy!") or a bad excitement ("Help!! Scary cat!!"). This is called "eye pinning".

Field of Vision - Sideways Eyes

Because keets' eyes are so far apart from each other, they often "point" an eye at an object to see it. You or I would point our nose at the object to see that object with both eyes. A keet would point the "side of her head" (i.e. one of her eyes) at the object to really focus on it.

See how far the eyes are from each other? They can't really see "forward". Each one takes care of one side of the parakeet. The left eye knows what's going on over in the left side of the room, and the right eye knows what's going on in the right side of the room.

For example, if a feather falls from my keet cage down to the ground, I will see all four keets turn their heads sideways and point one of their eyes at that feather as it falls down, down, down. It's really cute :).

There are videos on my website, if you'd like to see!

Health and Medical Information

Parakeets are fully dependent on you, their owner, to take proper care of them. All nutrition they receive is from your hands. Any safety risks that exist in their world are due to your actions (or inactions). Be sure to do your best to take good care of this life that is entrusted to you!

Keets are NOT disposable. They are very intelligent living creatures that can live up to fifteen years, can learn to call people by their name, and even sing full songs.

Please care for your keet with love and spend the time learning about safety issues!

Pesticides and Parakeets

Your home has some sort of a pest problem - maybe it's carpenter ants, maybe it's termites. You are considering having an exterminator come and blast the house with poison. The VERY FIRST THING you need to do is get your keet to safety LONG before this happens - and to keep your keet far, far away until the house is completely clean again.

Every single poison I have seen or researched has warnings on it to keep it away from ALL pets and small children. Think about this - if a small child can be affected, and a keet is only 1/20th of even a newborn's size, then the danger to a parakeet is astronomical. A keet can be affected by *incense* - never mind by a chemical specifically formulated to slay living creatures.

Poison doesn't just vanish after it's bombarded in a house, either. Even if you open all the doors and windows, remnants of that poison is going to cling to carpets, curtains, ceilings, you name it. A serious cleaning needs to be done before the house is safe for anybody to be in it. A tiny parakeet, with a tiny parakeet body stands little chance against poison. Remember the canaries in the coal mines? The canaries were brought in because they would keel over dead with only minute amounts of poison in the air. The canary's death would warn the miners to retreat. Not very nice for the canaries!

Parakeets have evolved to hide ALL symptoms of illness. Sick birds were the ones that predators would eat. So it's critical that you as the owner take all of the precautions. Just because the bird does not LOOK sick, does not mean the keet is not actually sick. Pesticides can cause nasty cancers and sicknesses. You might not know for another 5 years that a tumor is now growing inside your keet's body, making every single day miserable for your little bird.

Take this seriously. Pesticides are deadly. They should be avoided WHENEVER possible. We are only now learning how dangerous pesticides are for human beings. If you won't research this for your keet's health - research it for your OWN health. You only have one life to live on this planet, and if you damage your body, you won't get a new one

Pesticides Cause Asthma
Pesticide use is tied to causing asthma in children. Parakeets have very small lungs which we know are sensitive to "normal" substances like cigarette smoke and incense. It makes a great deal of sense that inhaling an *actual poison* that is meant to harm living tissue would seriously damage a parakeet's lungs.

Chemicals do not just flush out of a house after an hour or two. The chemicals cling to the fabrics of the home, and to the surfaces. A thorough cleaning needs to be done, to remove all traces of the poison before a pet or child can safely be returned to that environment.

Pesticides and Cancer
Take pesticides very seriously - not only for your keets, but for yourself. I would NEVER walk into a house that had been exterminated only a few hours ago.

The *New Media Explorer* reports: "Dozens of studies have now shown that several classes of pesticides are associated with brain cancers and leukemias in children"

"The risk of Wilms' tumor and lymphoma was elevated with professional extermination use during childhood and brain cancer was elevated with termite extermination during pregnancy"

"A recent study of pesticides and childhood brain cancers has revealed a strong relationship between brain cancers and compounds used to kill fleas and ticks"

Remember, these studies are done with HUMAN BEINGS who have large bodies. Little tiny keets only need a tiny speck of poison in their system to have disastrous results. Cancer is already a prime killer of parakeets in their middle age. Maybe the reason is that the humans that "care" for these keets subject them to pesticides - either in the home or on the lawn around the home. The poor little keets get a few specks of that poison in their system, and the tumor begins.

Pesticides Cause Death

Remember those children in the Philippines who died after eating food? It turns out they died because there were still pesticides on the food. Those were full sized kids that died. A parakeet would only need a minute trace of poison to die.

Whenever you feed any food to your parakeet - WASH IT THOROUGHLY. I know that I personally have gotten sick in the past by eating fruit that was not well washed, the pesticides still on the fruit did a serious number to me. I was nauseous and almost hallucinating. It took a full day for me to recover from that. Your keet has a TINY system and even the smallest hint of poison can seriously damage or kill your keet.

From a CNN Report on pesticides -
"Chlorpyrifos kills pests by disrupting normal nerve transmission, inhibiting an enzyme in the insect's nervous system. In humans, chlorpyrifos can cause headaches, blurred vision, nausea, convulsions, flu-like symptoms and even seizures. In extreme cases, it has been linked to quadriplegia, genetic damage, birth defects, immune-system abnormalities and death"

Pesticides Cause Miscarriages
If you have any doubt about how dangerous pesticides can be, read about the *Riverdeep Pesticide Information*: "A family has brought a lawsuit against an extermination company, claiming that a pesticide used in termite extermination in their home in 1996 is responsible for health problems among the family members--including difficulties breathing, persistent fever, and miscarriages. Tests run in 1998 by the state of New York and a private lab showed traces of chemicals used in the extermination job of two years earlier. The family moved out of the house."

If pesticides, TWO YEARS LATER, can cause death to a fetus, you better believe that pesticides can linger and cause serious issues and death for pets. Remember, poisons don't just "vanish" in 3-4 hours. Once you introduce pesticides into your home, you are faced with that poison acting on your body for whatever length of time you remain in the home.

Pesticides Contaminate for Years
If you think your home is safe to enter a few hours after an extermination or poison treatment, think again. Many studies have shown that the poisons are there - and

very active - for YEARS after the application.

From Safe2Use: "In a study reported by Dr. J. Milton Clark, Ph.D., at the School of Public Health, University of Illinois, half of the homes judged to have had a proper termiticide application had detectable air levels of chlordane, an average of 2.7 micrograms per cubic meter, months to years following the last application. The United States Environmental Protection Agency has often considered lifetime cancer risks exceeding one in a million as unacceptable. "

Chloradane is the traditional poison used for killing off pests - and this is INCREDIBLY dangerous.

TheBestControl.com says: "It has now been estimated that over 75% of all U. S. homes built prior to April, 1988 are still contaminated with significant levels of chlordane."

The poison doesn't just go away after application. It sits there, causing health problems for every inhabitant of the home. Why do you think termite people say "the bugs won't come back"? It's because the poison is still there.

I hope I've made my point. Never use pesticides in or around a house.

Natural Alternatives to Pesticides

You should NEVER put pesticides in your home or around your home unless it is the very last resort possible. The long term effects of pesticides are incredibly bad. They can cause cancers, miscarriages and death. There are many, many natural ways to deal with pests and fungus issues.

Keeping Pests Out

First, the only reason there are pests IN your house is that they got in somehow. Get sealing foam and gel, and go around and seal up the cracks and entries into your home. If pests are getting in, air is getting in too, which means your heating and cooling bills are skyrocketing. Many bad housekeeping practices also contribute to the problem. Do you have open cereal containers? Open containers of rice or flour? Tupperware is REALLY cheap. Seal up the food items in your pantries. If there is not food to eat, the pests and rodents will not come in!

All animals need water in order to live. If you have leaky faucets, leaky pipes or a leaky roof, you are asking for trouble. Not only do you help to keep pests alive, but you are also damaging your home. It's not that hard to patch these things. It just needs time and energy.

Many pests eat wood. NO wood should be in contact with the soil - you should have at least 18" between the bottom of the soil and where the wood begins. Your wood should be kept sealed and in good condition. All firewood and other lumber should be kept

FAR away from the house. NEVER bury wood or stumps anywhere near your home.

Slaying Existing Pests

What if the pests are already in your house? While you are doing the above tasks, get your hands on some silica gel or boric acid. These usually do the trick for critters in your home, without killing off your human and pet inhabitants. Many creatures are sensitive to garlic, soap and vinegar. Simply look up the thing you are trying to drive away, and find what the matching natural substance is.

Outside the Home

Why are you spraying poison around outside your home? It's going to drift right into the house, and be carried in on your shoes and clothing! Never mind the many natural birds and creatures that you are killing off. Look into natural solutions. Ladybugs for example eat up a TON of bad insects! Bats are wonderful at nibbling tons of mosquitos. A vinegar solution can handle many garden issues. Make sure you cover all garbage cans tightly and eliminate all standing water. That takes care of most of your issues with flying pests (flies, mosquitoes) right there.

Lawn Issues

If your lawn is unhealthy, it's your job to make it healthy! That means you water it properly, aerate it, fertilize it and maintain a proper pH. All of these things can be done with natural products.

Pest Repelling Naturally by Pest Type

If you've got a pest problem, do NOT turn to chemicals immediately. Poisons can literally pollute your home for years, and cause serious harm or even death to you and your pets! Here are some natural, safe alternatives. Remember that the primary key is to Tupperware all food, stop ALL drips and leaks, and close up any cracks or holes in your home.

Ants - wipe out trails with soapy water; red chili powder at homes. They hate walking across baby powder and chalk. Also repel with bay leaves, cloves, cucumber peelings.

Caterpillars - encourage frogs and toads

Cockroaches - cucumber skins, bay leaves

Fleas - rosemary, rye, fennel, pine needles, garlic

Flies - Lavender, clove, mint

Mice - peppermint

Mosquitoes - I have a TON of tips on mosquitos at my Birding Area

Moths - cinnamon, bay leaves, coriander, dill, lemon peel, black pepper. Basil is great for most flying bugs.

Nematodes - plant marigolds

Plant insects - wash leaves with soapy water, make sure they are planted far enough apart for natural aeration

Slugs - plant marigolds and onion

Snails - plant marigolds and onion

Ticks - rosemary, rye, fennel, pine needles

Healthy Parakeet Poops

There's a scene in *The Last Emperor* that's appropriate here. In the movie, the Chinese Emperor is a toddler being raised by civil servants. When he poops, a doctor actually collects the poop and examines it to make sure the toddler is healthy. When you're dealing with a patient that can't talk and explain what is wrong, looking at the poop is often the best way to figure out if everything is going well inside the person.

The same is true for a parakeet. Parakeets can't tell you when they have an upset tummy! You need to keep an eye on your parakeet's poops to make sure everything is going well.

Here's a picture of parakeet poop -

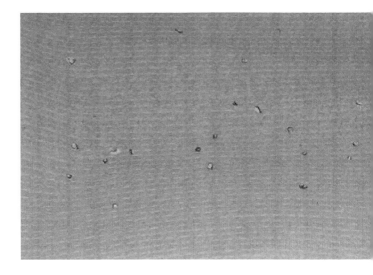

A parakeet doesn't pee. He just poops and the poop is sort of jello-like in consistency, so it has both the liquid and solid waste. It's about 1/4" across. There's an outer ring of dark color and an inner ring of white. Depending on how much veggies the parakeet ate during the day, the poop might be a bit watery or even green. But a parakeet should poop several times a day and while it can sometimes be runny from too much veggies, it shouldn't *always* be runny.

If you notice your parakeet has stopped pooping, or if the poops are very runny or strange looking, it's time to talk to a vet!

Parakeet poop is very easy to clean up - it dries into a hard little pellet that can easily be wiped up, and dissolves in regular water.

Radiograph / X-Rays

When parakeets are ill, often vets will take a radiograph of the parakeet to help diagnose the issue. First they will make the parakeet go unconscious with a very delicate gas which is even more sensitive than what they give to cats and dogs. The vet wants to make sure the fragile system of the parakeet is taken into account.

Then a system will send x-rays - a form of electromagnetic radiation - through the parakeet's body. The x-rays go through different types of body parts at different rates. They only go slightly through bone, but they go more easily through soft tissue. This lets you see the difference between bone and other body parts in the resulting image.

While the beams themselves are called X-Rays, the resulting image you get is called a radiograph.

When my 11 year old parakeet Santo suddenly was unable to put weight on her legs, we brought her to a vet who did a radiograph. This is the result. It turns out Santo had a tumor. You cannot see it well in this image. The second image shows the tumor more clearly as a grey oval shape in her lower abdomen.

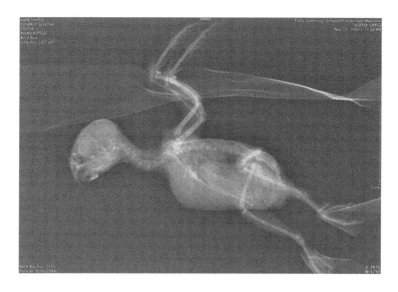

In a healthy bird, the bones would show as solid white on the edges (where they were very strong) and dark in the center, because birds' bones are hollow. This helps them to fly more easily. The vet said that because of the damage the tumor was doing, many of the bones here appear to be "solid white" which indicates a problem with calcium in the bones.

Here is the second image, with a note from the vet:

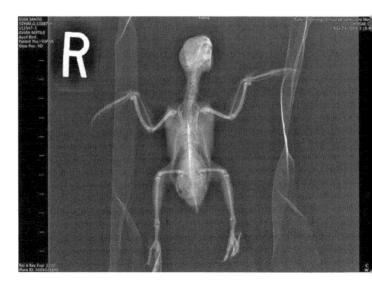

Please find attached the other view. yes, you are right the calcified bones is the problem and the fact that the air-sacs are compressed tell us that most likely a mass compresses them judging by the hepatic silhouette. there is clear loss of the hourglass shadow between the heart and the liver. this is due to the mass.

Lisa Shea

Ethoxyquin and Pet Food Preservatives

Before we even get into the ethoxyquin debate, we need to start with some basic information. First, keets, like humans, are meant to eat fresh food. We thrive best on fresh veggies, fresh milk, freshly caught fish, and fresh bread. I don't think anybody would contest that. If you freeze broccoli, ship it across the country, let it sit frozen for a year, thaw it out, and microwave it, you have already destroyed a TON of the vitamins that were in that original broccoli plant. It's a simple fact of life.

Second, many humans and pets make that trade-off daily for a number of reasons. We're too worn out from work to cook a real meal. We don't have enough money for an apartment with a stove - all we can afford is a microwave. We simply have no land available to have even a tiny garden. We are out at a jobsite where they do not allow us to bring in our own food, so all we can eat is the junk food / fast food there. Sometimes we can "help it". Sometimes we honestly can't. So there are going to be times that we MUST eat food with preservatives. Remember, preservatives are one of the only reasons that we can feed as many humans and pets as we can in modern days. If we didn't have preservatives, then most things you saw on the grocery shelves would be moldy and rotten.

OK, so we understand that healthy food is almost universally fresh food - but that we deliberately make trade-offs in life to buy NOT fresh food for whatever reason. In order to make that trade-off, we get foods with

preservatives so they are still edible when we get around to eating them. For example, if you got a can of cat food WITHOUT preservatives, then it would go rancid pretty quickly. So either you buy your meat fresh daily for your cat - or you buy canned food with preservatives. Most people choose the latter, for simplicity's sake.
Remember - if you DID want to feed your cat fresh meat daily, you could certainly do that! And your cat would really love it. It would just mean you had to go to and from the store each day, and pay the gas / grocery bills.

Ethoxyquin is a preservative that helps a food last longer. For example, in human food, ethoxyquin is used in paprika to keep the red color bright. It's used at about a volume of 100 parts per million (ppm). There is a FDA Page on ethoxyquin that says that you can start to harm rats if you feed them ethoxyquin in levels of 5,000 ppm or more. That's 50 times the rate used in human food. You could just as easily say that a glass of wine a day is fine for a human - but 50 glasses of wine in a day is harmful. Well, duh!

The Ethoxyquin Debate
OK, so here's the debate. We all agree that meat products / fatty products, if just put on a shelf, will go rancid. That would kill pretty much any animal, to eat that rancid item. We agree that most pet owners are just too lazy to go buy fresh meat for their pets every day :) We want convenience. So we have to put SOMETHING into the meat to keep it from going rancid quickly. That something is ethoxyquin. Ethoxyquin is a preservative that helps the meat stay edible. Right now, ethoxyquin is put into pet foods at a level of 150 parts per million. The FDA feels this is a safe level.

Some pet owners feel that this is too much - that at this level it causes liver damage in some pets. Studies are being done to see if the ethoxyquin is still able to "keep the meat safe" at lower levels. Remember, this is a serious trade-off we're considering here. On one hand we have meat that will go rancid and kill pets, if it is not made safe. On the other hand, we have a few pets that can get liver damage, if they get too much ethoxyquin. So at what point do we lover the ethoxyquin levels so *no* pet ever gets liver damage - vs a number of pets now get poisoned by rancid meats.

Yes, there are going to be organic pet food makers who claim that organic food is better. And you know what, I agree with them. If you can get fresh food for your pet, it's always going to be best. I feed my keets fresh lettuce. That is much better than buying them dried, preserved lettuce bits that were shipped to me from China. I feed my keets fresh carrots which are better than feeding them dried preserved carrot bits from Venezuela. If you are willing to get fresh, unpreserved food for your pet and feed him daily - AVOIDING ALL CHANCE OF RANCID / BAD FOOD - then you are a great pet owner and should be pleased with yourself. However, most pet owners will NOT go through this trouble. They will buy fresh food, let it sit around and then feed the going-rancid or going-moldy food to the pet figuring it's "close enough". The pet then gets food poisoning and dies.

You have to be completely realistic here. You only have X hours in your day you are willing to devote to your pet. You only have Y budget of money. If you were a millionaire and had a special Pet-Servant to care for your pet, then that pet-servant could run to the store to

167

fetch fresh food every day. The pet-servant could carry the food in a special cooler that was sterile, and make sure the pet received the freshest, best, most nutritious food around. That way the food would be infection-free and your pet would be the healthiest pet in your entire state, probably.

But few of us are millionaires and few of us can spend the hours each week necessary to get fresh food. We are going to shop at most once a week for our pet, and that food has to last all week. We are not going to be super sterile about how we store that food. A pet's body is usually much smaller than ours - so if they get a small amount of "bad food" it could kill them. To their body, that is still a large amount. So to me, preservatives are a critical way that most of us can ensure our pets stay fed with at least some reassurance that the food hasn't rotted. But if you have the money and time, by all means spend more for organic food, and make sure you get it fresh, frequently, because it's going to go bad quickly. That is the responsibility you take on when you make that choice for your pet's diet.

Ascaris and Capillaris Worms

Worms in birds are just like worms in dogs, cats, humans and other creatures. They live in the intestinal tract of the animal and feed off of the nutrition the animal is supposed to be getting. Sometimes you may actually see little worms in the poop of the bird and around their tail feathers, but other times you may just notice that the bird is acting lethargic and slow.

If you suspect worms, SEE YOUR VET. Only your vet can handle this problem and diagnose it properly.

Tumors and Cancer

As I mention in several of my FAQ pages, tumors are unfortunately common in parakeets. A healthy parakeet might live to be 15 or 20 years old. Many parakeets, though, only make it to around 7-9 years before they develop a tumor and die. A tumor is a 'lump' of cancer, just like humans get cancer and tumors. With humans, there are serious drugs and radiation involved in trying to beat cancer, and many times (if not most of the time) the treatment is unsuccessful. Cancer is still a very powerful foe in our modern world.

Because the cancer is a physical lump growing inside the parakeet's body, and because the body is so tiny to begin with, it is often practically impossible to just "remove" the tumor. Remember, with human beings they can't just cut out the tumor and have the entire tumor removed, usually. Usually they have to give strong doses of medicine as well as radiation before they get rid of all of the cancer - if they can even achieve it. If a woman has breast cancer, even if they lop off the entire breast, there is still often cancer 'bits' in her system that remain.

Since parakeets do not have easily removable body parts, and since the tumor is usually deep within them, unfortunately the best you can usually do is allow them to die peacefully vs having them linger slowly in pain as the cancer slowly kills them.

X-Rays and blood tests can usually verify that cancer is indeed the problem with your keet, rather than some other ailment. If you don't see a lump somewhere, the cancer could still be inside them and causing them not to eat well, or walk well, or so on.

There are rare instances where the cancerous tumor / lump is 100% on the edge of the body - i.e. a lump at the end of their wing. In this case it can be possible to cut off the lump and still have the parakeet survive. It will be expensive, but it might work. Just remember that surgery is always risky, and the bird could still die from complications.

I have had two birds develop known tumors. Here is more information about each situation, to help you understand how tumors can vary.

Pinto's Tumor

Pinto was acquired in December 1998 as a hand raised baby, so she was born late October / early November 1998. She came from a pet store in Natick MA. She and our year-older green parakeet Nazo - both females from that same breeder - hit it off famously and were partners for their entire lives, until Nazo died in 2008. Pinto became a bit more lonely and cranky after that. We did have two other parakeets - Santo and Ivory - but they had paired up meaning Pinto was now the "odd parakeet out". She had a flock, but she no longer had a partner.

Pinto was always the large parakeet of the four. We almost thought she had some English parakeet in her. She was always the football-player-shaped one compared with the others who were more svelte. So we never thought anything of it when Pinto seemed a bit larger than the rest.

Then in late October 2009, while Pinto was going through a molt and taking lots of baths, we saw that she had an actual bulge in her rear area. These next few photos show when we really noticed it. It was the combination of the no-feathers and the super-wet body which made it very apparent that she had an unnatural bulge showing now. I realize her feathers look a bit ratty here but it is primarily that she had gotten soaking wet, which is when we could really see her bulge.

Note - these might look a bit gross. It's important to know what these things look like, so you can watch for signs on your own pet. Keep in mind that she's not "hurt" in these images. She just has a bump in her body.

It's like you having a wart on your hand. It's just a bump. If it looks a bit "slimy" that's just that she's wet from her bath.

Parakeets

My first thought was that Pinto was egg bound. The keets are all female, but that hasn't stopped them from thinking they can create babies with each other and we do occasionally get eggs (infertile of course). I was, of course, really worried. Egg binding is a serious condition and can kill a keet off very quickly. I took Pinto upstairs to the sink, let her rest in warm water, used olive oil on the area, and she seemed to treat it as a luxury spa. She enjoyed the attention greatly. But it became apparent fairly quickly that this was not an egg and it wasn't coming out. Time for a vet.

I took Pinto in to the vet the first few days of November. The vet decided fairly quickly that this was a tumor and it was inoperable. She said that she could do an x-ray to confirm, but that the x-ray procedure would probably kill Pinto and since it would just show that Pinto had an inoperable tumor, there would be little gain. Instead she pressured me very hard to simply kill Pinto right there, since she wasn't going to last more than a week or two anyway. I felt as if the process was fairly callous.

Add onto that the "exit procedure." After the vet was done, they sent in an intern with a folder of information for me and she tried to start selling me on buying parakeet pellet food and such. Here I am with a sick parakeet apparently "on death's door" and they are pressuring me to buy food? Not good at all.

I was of course crying the whole way home and was convinced poor Pinto was on her last breath. I wondered if I had been selfish to keep Pinto alive, if she was going to have a miserable week or two of her last hours. I snuggled with Pinto when I got home and doted on her. But in a day or two it was fairly obvious that Pinto was NOT on her last few hours. She was happy, chirping, playing with the other keets and as lively as she'd always been. I do realize that keets try to hide their symptoms so they will not be predated on in the wild. However, close observation made it clear Pinto was not pretending for show, that she really was enjoying her treats and seeking out fun.

Once her feathers grew back in from the molt, she

looked fairly normal too. These photos below are taken AFTER the above ones - so she still has the bulge, but they're hidden under her feathers.

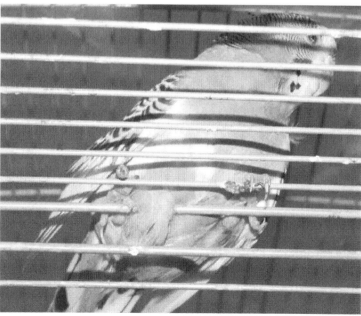

Not only that, but a month and a half later (long after her "expiration date" set by that vet) by a very strange twist of fate Santo died almost instantly from a hidden tumor. So while Pinto had this obvious, pushing-out tumor which she lived with fine, Santo had an internal tumor which we noticed when her legs began to fail and three days later she was gone. So it goes to show how very differently tumors can present themselves.

Throughout December and January Pinto was alive and well, still with the tumor, and was now extremely happy being the "partner" of Ivory. So rather than her last memories being of the "odd bird out" without a partner, her last memories were of being snuggled and preened. When she finally did head into her final days, they were peaceful, calm, and with us.

Santo's Tumor

Blue Parakeet Santo was a lovely blue parakeet who was born in late December 1998. Santo lived a very happy life in our "flock of four", which were all female parakeets. Santo "paired" with Ivory, also female, and they spent a lot of time together. Santo and Ivory very actively wanted to make baby parakeets but of course it was not meant to be. Still they tried, daily, very actively. When Nazo passed away, and then Pinto became very ill with a tumor, it seemed like Santo and Ivory would be going strong for many years to come.

Of the four parakeets, Santo, Nazo, and Pinto all

came from a breeder in Natick MA, from different clutches. Ivory was adopted from a family member, from an entirely different location.

It was November 2009 when Pinto's tumor became serious, and we were spending all of our time caring for Pinto. Santo and Ivory were doing their thing, amazingly active and acrobatic. We were worried that the two were "harassing" Pinto a bit, which is normal keet behavior when there is an ill keet in the flock. We tried to keep a close eye on them so they could be together without Pinto getting hurt. Any time we tried to remove Pinto from the flock she got very upset and we decided supervised visits were the best way to go.

Then all of a sudden we came into the room to find Santo "splayed" on the front drawbridge of the cage, as in she had her body sitting flat down on the drawbridge and her feet out to either side. It seemed that she could put weight on one of her legs but not the other. We immediately thought that Santo and Pinto had gotten into a tussle and that Pinto had done something serious to Santo's leg, and given it a wrench. Or maybe Santo had been climbing in the cage and had somehow fallen and caught herself by her leg, twisting it. Nothing looked broken at all. There was no blood at all. The claw could still clutch. She just couldn't put any weight on the leg.

We promptly put Santo into the smaller travel cage and layered the bottom of it with pine pellets so she could drag herself to her food and water without having to climb at all. She had softness beneath her wherever she went. We really hoped that it was a temporary sprain - as happens sometimes - and watched for any signs that she was putting weight on it. But it soon was apparent that this was not a small wrench and we took her in to the vet. Interestingly while she was at home it seemed like she could use one leg - but at the vet's it was more clear that she really couldn't put weight on either leg.

To my surprise, the vet immediately thought it might be a tumor. There was NO sign, looking at Santo from the outside that there was any tumor at all in her. Her body was completely normal shaped. To me it seemed only that her legs were not working. But the vet did some tests and found that her legs were fine, but they could no longer support the body weight. What happens commonly is a tumor forms inside and presses against the sciatic nerve. Once that happens, the keet cannot support her weight any more. Trying to extricate this kind of a tumor is nearly impossible.

They asked me if I wanted to do an x-ray to confirm, in case it was something else that COULD be fixed. I said yes. They took Santo out for the x-ray. Unfortunately, being anesthetized was too much for the past-11 year old parakeet, and Santo passed away in her sleep. Since she had lost the use of both legs, it probably was for the best.

Note: Cancer vs Tumor

A medical doctor sent me this clarification - please read:

"A tumor is a group of cells that have abnormally proliferated. Cancer represents those tumor cells that not only have abnormally proliferated, but they have lost the normal function of "programmed cell death" and often have lost many of the inherent normal features of the once normal cell that has transformed. They proliferate, unregulated, and abnormally, and will invade local tissues and possibly metastasize to other sites in the body.

Not all tumors are cancer, in fact many are benign. That means they just stay where they are and do not have the ability to transform into cancer no matter how big they get.

Some cancers can be cured - for instance a local cancer that is completely resected, or some types of cancer that are extremely sensitive to chemotherapy such as testicular cancer or some childhood leukemias. When we cannot see any cancer but do not know if there is cancer we cannot say, we say the cancer is in remission, which means there is no clinically evident disease.

Obviously this is well beyond the scope of the parakeet web site - but I wanted to be sure that you understood the subtleties."

Coccidiosis

Coccidiosis is an illness named after the protozoan parasite which causes it, named *Eimeria*. Coccidiosis can affect not only parakeets but other birds, cats, dogs, people, cows, goats, you name it. Some bird owners theorize that all parakeets actually have a small amount of *Eimeria* in them - and that it is only the birds that are poorly taken care of that get symptoms and sick because of it. It's like the "common cold". Most of us are exposed regularly to this, but only those of us who are weak or temporarily immune-impaired that tend to get sick.

In parakeets, coccidiosis is usually noticed by lethargic behavior and very wet, runny droppings. Sometimes there is a bit of blood in the droppings as well. Because the droppings are so moist, you might also note that the feathers around your parakeet's rear end look "dirty".

Note that wet droppings can also be caused by a juicy diet such as lots of lettuce or tomatoes. So try putting your parakeet just on seeds for a few days and see if the problem continues.

If it does, you need to take your pet to a vet immediately. The vet will need a microscope to know for sure what is going on, and will give you the medicine to treat it.

Egg Binding

All female parakeets can lay eggs, whether or not a male is around. Think of chickens. Female chickens can mate with a male rooster and lay eggs that hatch into baby chicks (which are very cute!). Female chickens can ALSO lay eggs without mating with a male rooster - those eggs get gathered up and sent to the grocery store, where we eat them for breakfast. The eggs we get at the supermarket don't have chicks in them, they'll never turn into chickens. They are unfertilized eggs. So female parakeets can lay eggs that are fertilized (hatchable) if males are around. They can also lay eggs that are unfertilized if no males are around but they feel like egg laying.

I currently have 3 female parakeets that are all 8 and 7 years old. They have NEVER laid an egg. But I know of other people who have a female parakeet in a cage with a nest and a mirror, and she "thinks" she has a husband, so she lays eggs. It does happen.

Usually there's no issue - if you know there is no male around, simply remove the eggs before they go rotten. If there IS a male around, you definitely need to read all of my pages on breeding, talk to breeders in the area, talk to your vet, and be very well prepared for the consequences. Breeding parakeets is not a task to take lightly, it is very serious.

But there are times that a hen (female parakeet) can get "egg bound." This means that she makes an egg, but the egg gets stuck as it slides out of her. Sometimes this is because she's overweight and the extra fat is blocking the egg channel. Other times it is because she has a poor diet and the egg isn't strong enough to slide through smoothly. You might see a bulge at the back end of the bird, see it sitting in one spot and straining as it tries to pass the egg.

If this activity has just begun, you can try making sure the room is nice and warm. Warm muscles are generally loose muscles and that helps out. Don't *heat* the bird, just make sure it isn't cold or cool. Also, if she is hand trained (which hopefully she is by now!!) get a little cooking oil and rub it on her rear end. That might help the egg slip out.

But if neither of these work, call a vet immediately to get help with this.

Gout - uric acid buildup

Gout is the body's inability to get rid of uric acid - either because the kidneys do not efficiently get rid of the normal amounts, or because a disorder causes the body to produce it too much.

Genetics have an effect on gout, and overeating and alcohol consumption also increase the risk for gout.

So for a parakeet, if your keet develops gout, it has to do probably with its diet. Try to give the keet a more healthy, balanced diet. If the issue is genetic, then talk with your vet about what sort of a diet can at least ease the issue.

Ornithosis - Psittacosis

Ornithosis is the name of an avian disease that parakeets can pass along to humans. The main symptoms are seen in the parakeet's eyes - they will have tears flowing from their eyes and will blink a lot to try to clear them. In humans, the symptoms are like a serious flu or pneumonia - headache, fever, chills, etc.

This disease is also called psittacosis, "parrot fever" or "parrot disease".

If you suspect your keet has ornithosis, SEE YOUR VET. Only your vet can handle this problem and diagnose it properly.

Rectal Prolapse

Innards Protruding from the Parakeet's Rear End

Parakeets have a digestive system much like a human's. Food goes into the parakeet's mouth. It goes down to her stomach. It is digested in the stomach, and then sent through the intestines. Whatever is left then comes out the parakeet's rear end in a poop.

A parakeet's intestines can become weakened for two main reasons. First, the keet's intestines can become weak because she doesn't get enough nutrients (i.e. is on a seed-only diet). Second, the keet can become infested with parasites who in essence suck away the nutrients before the bird can use them. Either way, the intestines no longer hold in place well and in essence 'slide out' the end hole, bulging there. It can look like a red marble stuck out the rear end of the parakeet.

This is of course not healthy for the bird! You need to bring the parakeet to a vet right away. The vet will gently get the innards back into the bird where they belong, and then stitch the hole mostly closed so that the innards don't fit out any more. Also, of course, the intestines need to be strengthened so they don't have this problem in the future - by a proper diet and by removal of parasites (if there were some).

Scaly Face - Mycosis

Mites are tiny creatures that live on another animal and use that animal's blood to stay alive. Most of us know about ticks and how they latch onto humans. Mites are the same, only smaller.

One disorder parakeets can get from mites is called scaly face, or mycosis. This is usually seen by a brown scaly look to the skin around the beak or cere (nose) of the parakeet. If you let the mites continue, they will multiply and more and more of the skin will get bumpy, brown and nasty looking. This can also happen to a keet's feet.

If you see this begin to happen, TALK TO A VET. You need to get medicine to get this under control right away, before it spreads to the rest of the bird.

Sour Crop - Stomach Ache

Calling an illness "sour crop" is sort of like saying someone has a "tummy ache" - it's a very general term for something being off with the stomach. The crop of a bird is its belly. So a sour crop is anything that causes a bird to eat less well or to stop eating.

A sour crop can be caused just like with humans by eating something that isn't great for you. A bird eating random objects it finds around the house can get an upset stomach. A bird that is force-fed too much food (say a baby bird that a parent is overzealous with) or one that gets food that is too hot or cold can end up with an upset tummy too.

How to solve it? Well, don't do whatever you did to the bird again :). Usually the situation will sort itself out naturally. If something is truly stuck in the bird's stomach, take it to a vet for assistance.

Note that sometimes illnesses can also make a bird not feel like eating - just like with humans. In these cases the sour crop is just a side effect of something else is wrong. You would need to fix the real problem in those situations for the bird to feel hungry again.

Vertigo - stargazing, twirling

Vertigo in humans is when they lose their sense of balance. The same thing can happen to a bird - and since a bird just has two little feet clutching onto a perch, it can cause the bird to fall down or act dizzy. The bird can also do twisting motions with his head, as he tries to find a balance.

In general, vertigo is considered to be a vitamin problem. Usually giving multivitamins for a week will sort it out, if it's just a recent problem. If you let this issue go for too long, then it will of course take longer to cure.

Of course in humans vertigo can be caused by many different things, so it's true for birds too. If a bird got hit on the head sharply, they could have vertigo issues.

Another situation that causes vertigo is overfeeding. The thought is that either worms begin to infest the bird, or that the blood flow is disrupted by the heaviness of the bird.

If you don't believe a blow to the head was involved, then make sure that your bird has a very balanced set of food, with vitamins added.

Vomiting

First, note that vomiting is far different from regurgitation. When a parakeet regurgitates, it gently brings up partially digested food, often as a sign of love. This is how parent parakeets feed their babies, and how parakeets that are in love feed each other. This often happens when a parakeet falls in love with you the owner, too. The parakeet might bob their head a bit, and then 'bring up' a few seeds for you. Tell your parakeet that she is a good girl and put the seeds in the trash if this happens :)

However, just like humans vomit when their tummies hurt, parakeets vomit too. A real "vomit" involves the stomach contents spewing out of the parakeet's mouth and nose and often all over the cage.

Why do parakeets vomit? You might as well ask why humans vomit. Sometimes it's because we eat something that is bad for us - bad food, toys, whatever. Sometimes it's because we have a cold and the vomiting is just a part of the sickness. Sometimes it's because we inhaled bad fumes and the fumes made us ill. Sometimes it's that we have a much more serious problem - like a tumor - and the vomiting is a sign that something is wrong with our system.

So the same is true with a parakeet. Something caused the vomit, but the vomit is not "the problem". It's just a symptom. First, go with the assumption that it was something they ate - either a strange object or bad food. Clean out their cage and get them fresh, healthy food, fresh water and clean linings. Check the temperature around the cage to make sure it's warm - not hot or cold - with no breezes. Make sure they're covered at night and have a full 8 hours of dark sleep. If it was a one-time ingestion problem or a cold, this should help them get over it.

Make sure you're not using Teflon cookware and that nobody is smoking or lighting incense or using carpet cleaner around the cage. That should take care of any fume issues.

If the parakeet still gets sick again, take him in to a vet. Something more serious might be wrong, and the doctor can run the tests to figure out what it is.

Red Mites, Feather Mites, Scaly Face Mites

Mites are tiny creatures that live on another animal and use that animal's blood to stay alive. Most of us know about ticks and how they latch onto humans. Mites are the same, only smaller.

Parakeets tend to get three different types of mites:

* Red Mites
* Feather Mites
* Scaly Face Mites

Mites don't just spring out of the earth. Most parakeets that get mites get them from a badly cared for pet shop. This is part of why it's critical to buy only from a reputable dealer - and to take your parakeet immediately to a vet for a checkup. If your parakeet is safe at that point, the likelihood of it spontaneously developing mites later on is slim.

Sometimes you can see the mites as moving black or red dots on the parakeet. Note that parakeets do grow in new feathers, so don't mistake an incoming new feather (especially on the top of the keet's head) for a mite. If your keet has mites, it will tend to be slow and sluggish. Their blood is being weakened by this parasite.

While there are mite sprays on the market, I personally would never start randomly spraying a pet without knowing for sure what is going on. It COULD be mites, or it could be something more serious. Those sprays that they sell are not exactly "healthy" for living things! If it is NOT mites that your keet has, you could in fact make them even worse by forcing them to live in a cloud of toxic smoke.

So talk to your vet, and get an appointment. Your vet will know how to handle the situation and return your keet to its normal, happy self!

When a Keet Passes Away

It's always a sad thing when a parakeet passes away. A keet can live for up to twenty years, so for a young adult the keet may literally have been a member of the household for their entire lifetime. Not only is it hard on the human beings in the house, but it's also hard on any remaining keets in the cage.

A period of mourning is natural, of course, as when any living creature passes away. If it helps, make a memorial to the keet - put out photos of the keet, put up a website with pictures. Share stories. Talk on our forum to let us know what a wonderful keet it was.

Keep in mind that life and death are very natural things, and they happen. Your keet was at one point born from a little egg, springing into life. She lived her life and reached the end, and had to pass away again. It is the cycle of things. When you are ready, consider getting another keet, to share all of the knowledge and wisdom and love you have learned about keets with a new, fluffy little friend. You undoubtedly have at this point a nice cage, food, and the experience necessary to take great care of a little parakeet. There is probably the perfect keet waiting for you at your local pet store or breeder's home that would be a perfect companion for you.

For some people, they are ready to get the new keet in a few days. Others take a few weeks before you are ready. Don't rush it - but don't necessarily spend months and months mourning the lost keet. The keet will live on in your memory, and the time she spent with you is now valuable in that you can be an even better owner to the new keet in your life!

If you are going to introduce a new keet into an existing flock of birds, make sure you read my pages on adding a second bird. Also, if your bird died an unusual death, such as poisoning, make sure you take care of any environmental issues (i.e. removing all Teflon pans from the house, etc.) before getting the new bird.

Journal of Health and Skills

Keeping a parakeet journal can be critical in watching over the health of your parakeet. It can also be great fun, as you write down the new skills and words that your parakeet learns over time, to look back over his or her progress. While it's best to take your parakeet in to a nearby bird vet each year for checkups, just like you do with a cat or dog, many people don't do that. You need to at least watch over your parakeet's health on your own, and watch out for any danger signs that something is wrong.

It's best to keep the journal right by the cage with a pen, so it's always within reach. The more notes you take, the more likely you are to catch something small before it becomes a big problem. Things you should take note of are:

* Date/time of entry
* General energy level of parakeet
* Any problems with feathers, molting, bare spots, itching
* Any strange textures/colors of poops (greenish? yellowish? watery? none at all?)
* Eating problems (seeds look untouched?)

The energy level is especially important with a parakeet. Yes, they take lots of naps during the day, so sometimes they are sleepy and at other times they're very active. But parakeets are taught by nature never to "seem" really sick. Predators go after sick animals. So they try their best to not look sick even if they're really ill. The only change you might see is a general listlessness, a lack of interest when you come by, a lack of interest when you play music. Watch for those subtle changes - it could be a sign of something serious.

Journals are great for medical reasons, but they're also great just for general fun. Parakeets are INCREDIBLY smart birds and can learn to do acrobatic tricks, they can learn to mimic noises around them and many can even learn to talk. They're smart enough to learn peoples' names and use them properly. Keep notes on the words and skills your parakeet learns, and be sure to reward your bird at each new skill! Birds thrive on attention and the more you lavish your keet with love, the more your keet will try even harder to do something even cooler the next time around.

Emergencies

By their very nature, emergencies can't be planned for. That's why it's critical to have a vet's number posted next to the cage and a stocked medical kit on hand. That way when the event happens you're there and ready to take the next step.

Here's a few situations that you'll want to be prepared for.

Lisa Shea

Getting Back an Escaped Budgie

It's every bird owner's nightmare. You made sure your budgie was finger-trained. You made sure your budgie was only let out when all doors and windows were closed. You were very careful about letting everyone in the house know that the budgie was out and loose. You took your ownership responsibility very serious and protected your little pet.

But then SOMETHING happened. Maybe your Aunt Edna stopped by for a visit and walked right in, and your budgie flew out the door! Maybe a fire alarm went off and there was no way to get the budgie back into its cage before you had to leave the house and get to safety. Now your budgie is out in the cold, cruel world and doesn't know what to do. How do you get your budgie to return to you?

It is REALLY important that you get your budgie to return home to you. Parakeets are not equipped to handle the outside world, except maybe in Florida where they have set up small colonies. There are many predators out in the world that eat budgies. Their bodies aren't meant to handle the hot heats and frigid night that most of the world has. There aren't foods for them to easily eat just lying around. Budgies are domesticated pets that need an owner to care for them.

Your budgie knows its cage is a place of safety, a place that provides shelter, food, drink and love. So the most important thing to do is put the budgie's cage out in the middle of the lawn, maybe up on a table so it is easy to see. Fill it with food and water and leave the door open. Then put a chair nearby and start calling to your budgie. If you can't sit there for long, make a looping tape of your voice and play it.

Birds naturally fly high when they are scared, and can easily get disoriented in a strange place. Your bird may be high up in the treetops a half mile away, frightened and with no idea of how to get "home". The bird will hear your voice and fly towards it. When the bird sees its cage, it will be happy and fly down to it, to safety.

If you try this for a week and your budgie hasn't returned, then sadly, it probably has fallen victim to the harsh laws of nature. I would get another budgie - but be sure to take VERY GOOD CARE of this one! A budgie is a living creature that can live 15 years or more. Budgies can talk, they can fall in love with humans, they can be loyal companions. All they ask for in return is that you care well for them and keep them safe. Never giving them an opportunity to escape is one of your most important tasks!

Power Failures

Power failures are a fact of life. Anywhere that gets electrical power can - and most undoubtedly will - have power failures. Cars hit poles and knock them down. Computers go awry and mess up at power stations. Winter storms knock down trees, ice forms on power lines. You name it, it happens somewhere. The key is not to wait until the emergency strikes to start to prepare for it!

First, power failures often knock out water. Water is one of those most necessary things in life, far more important than food. So always have a gallon or two of bottled water in the basement. Change it out every year or two so that the water is always fairly fresh. If it's a situation where you expect power might fail - like a winter storm is bearing down on you - then fill up your sinks and bathtub with water. That way you have emergency water to keep you going for a few days.

Next, food. You should always have at least a week of food in the house, for you and for your pets. That way if the roads become impassable for some reason you don't have to worry about going out to get more. Don't let your food run down to the dregs before you go to get more. Always keep a set of seed or pellets or whatever your main food item is.

Make sure you have battery powered lamps - as well as a few shake-to-activate ones. You definitely do NOT want to have flame based lights going in an emergency system. Yes, it might seem romantic - but take a look at the statistics of how many houses burn down due to candles and other flame based lighting. If you already have an emergency going on, the last thing you want is to add a burning house to that mix. Also, if you read the article below on candles and parakeets you'll find that they simply aren't good to have near parakeets.

Make sure your battery powered lamps are somewhere easy to get to. The best way is usually to have a few of the hand-wind ones in key locations - by the bed, in a main desk, in the kitchen. That way one is very close and is guaranteed to make light. That will let you get to wherever you have the other ones stored.

It hopefully goes without saying that you really should not be letting your parakeet out at all during this period. There are all sorts of things that could happen. You might need to leave your house and relocated. You might really need to move to another room. Your keets will be fine being in their cage for a few days.

Summer
In the summer, the issue is that things can get too hot. Find the breeziest part of the house, and set the cage up there - but use light sheets so that the breeze isn't blowing ON the keets. Use hand fans if necessary to add some breeze. Make sure you have LOTS of water available to hydrate. Use curtains to block the sun from coming into the house.

Winter
Winter usually poses the more challenging issue. Human beings can layer on more clothes, and can snuggle together for warmth. Keets do have a warm layer of feathers, but that only gets them so far.

It's tempting to use gas powered type of heater - but the fumes they put out are not good for little lungs. Instead, get everyone to sleep in one room. The body warmth is a huge part of keeping a room warm. Do the normal wintry types of house-sealing activities. Cover the windows with plastic, then with a layer or two of thick fabric. Seal all drafts with towels. If you have a fireplace, and you must use it, keep the keets at the far end so they get as little soot as possible in their lungs. Cover their cage with a heavy fabric to keep out all drafts and so they can conserve their own heat. Have a little "snuggly tube" of fabric in the cage for them to snuggle in. Even if your keet doesn't normally use one, have one in a drawer to use for this emergency. If it gets really cold, then occasionally take the keet out of the cage - I know I said not to but this is an emergency - and hold the keet against you to restore their body warmth. Then once they're "recharged" they can fluff up in their cage and go for a while longer.

Get pizza stones, ceramic bricks or any other stones and heat them up with whatever options you have, and put them beneath the cage. The heat will rise through the cage to help out. Don't ever put anything hot into the cage, though.

Heat their water to a *lukewarm* (never hot!) temperature so that the water helps to warm them from inside. Just like humans drink tea and hot cocoa, parakeets can drink warm water to help.

Make sure you always have a well-stocked medical kit, so that no matter what happens, you are ready for emergencies.

Long Term Parakeet Care

Parakeets live for fifteen years or even longer. Set in place a happy, healthy routine from the very beginning, and it will be easy for your parakeet to become a treasured part of your daily life!

Bath-time

Many bird owners don't realize how much birds love to take baths, either because they don't offer bathtubs to their birds, or because they leave the bathtubs in the cages, where they get grungy. Baths are important not only for the bird's sunny disposition, but also for their health.

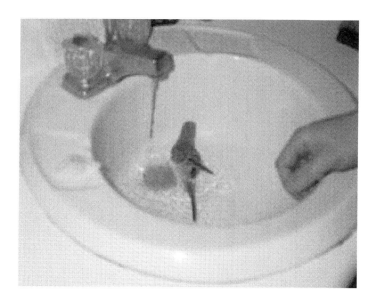

Birds in the wild naturally take baths in puddles or by the edges of water areas. They enjoy this a great bit, splashing around in the water, and it of course helps keep their feathers clean.

If you have a pet bird, you should give it this same opportunity. Find a bathtub that is large enough to hold your bird, but shallow enough that its head is still above water when it stands in it. At least once a week, fill the bath with tepid (NOT hot or cold) water, and put the bath somewhere that the bird feels safe getting into.

Many birds will immediately hop into the bath, while others might need time to get used to the tub. They'll open their feathers wide to get water underneath, and splash around. When they're done, be sure they have a warm, non-breezy place to dry off.

You might even find your birds enjoy other bathing areas. My parakeets love to splash under a slowly-running faucet in the sink, playing in the gentle, lukewarm water stream. One even hops on my shoulder when I take a shower myself, playing in the water that's running off my head!

On a related note, NEVER make water a punishment for a bird - don't spray or mist them when you wish to punish them (as some people do with cats). A bird should relish playing in water, drinking water, and enjoying water. To make it even remotely a 'bad thing' is going to harm your bird's ability to keep clean and hydrated.

See if you can make bathing another fun part of your shared life with your birds. They'll thank you for it. If you don't currently have a parakeet bathtub, they're available at any pet store near you

Lisa Shea

How to Get your Keet to Bathe

First, your bird actually DOES naturally want to bathe. Just about every parakeet is happy when she hears the sound of running water. Birds instinctively want to keep their feathers clean and love to jump around in puddles. The problem is that there aren't any puddles in your house or in her cage. There are only strangely shaped water containers. So your job is to teach her that these water containers (i.e. tiny bathtubs and sinks) are not dangerous.

Start with a small bathtub, or a small dish. It should be something that easily fits into her cage and can be taken in and out. Your aim at the beginning isn't even to get her IN the tub. It's simply to teach her that this object is not a scary one. Each day, when you change her food and water, change the water in the tub. Make sure it's lukewarm. She is just learning that the tub is an OK, normal object in her life.

If your parakeet is not yet hand trained, you have to wait to progress until she is. Once she's hand trained and the bathtub has been in her cage for around 2 weeks, you're ready to move along to the next part.

Now, one of the times that you are refilling the tub, don't just put it back onto the bottom of the cage. Instead, hold it in one hand and with the other, reach in and get your keet on your finger. If she's hand trained, she'll hop on. Now SLOWLY bring the bathtub and the bird towards each other, keeping the tub low so that she can watch it approach. This is not a fast scary thing. It is a "I have a friend for you to meet" movement. Talk to her in a calm tone so she knows this is not scary. She might fly away the first time or two, but soon she'll get used to this. After all, she sees water in the tub. The tub is a normal part of her cage now. She knows that she drinks water every day.

Once she is able to be next to the tub, she might take a little sip of water. Press the tub gently against her chest and say "up" just like you do with a perch during hand training. She should get onto the edge of the tub. Again it might take a few days to get her to do this, but eventually she will. Just be patient and keep at it.

Once she's ON the tub she should pretty much decide to hop in or at least splash a bit on her own. If the water is nice and warm, it's very inviting to a parakeet. Once you get over that initial hurdle of having her go into it, she'll want to go in frequently after that!

Many birds love to bathe daily, just like humans do. Be sure to let your bird have somewhere warm and dry to dry off! Birds can catch cold rather easily.

If you don't currently have a parakeet bathtub, they're available at any pet store near you

Showers and a Parakeet

This works best if you have a see-through shower curtain, because while your keet might be afraid of a shower, your keet definitely enjoys doing fun things with you. Set up the shower head to point straight down, so you can leave the curtain partially open. Now set up a perch for your keet so she can sit and watch you.

The first few times you try this, don't try to get your bird near the shower. The first aim is just to get your bird used to the room itself, to the sounds and noises. Set your keet down on the perch, then take your shower as usual. Be sure to talk to your bird and let her know you are having fun in there.

After 3-4 times of just getting the keet used to the room, now it's time to move things along. Start the water running as usual, at a nice lukewarm temperature. Walk towards the shower, talking soothingly to the keet. If she flies over to her perch, that's fine. Let her be there. Each time, she should let you get closer and closer to the water, because she understands that this is a normal situation to be in. Eventually she will let you be in the shower, with her on your finger.

The main stream is usually too strong for a keet, so there are several options that seem to work well. One is to cup your hands together, to catch water in them. Then your keet can splash around in your cupped hands as if it was a bathtub. Another technique is to let water run off your body, and put your finger-perch underneath that more gentle stream.

Your keet might just take a quick dunk or two, or might play in the water until she is completely soaked.

Either way, don't force the keet to stay, but do play with her for as long as she wants to. Often the keet will fly up to the curtain rod to take a break, then fly down again for more splashing. Be sure to keep an eye on the keet - a soaking wet keet will have trouble flying, and might need help in getting back to a regular perch area.

When you're done, remember that a soaking wet bird can catch a chill if brought out into a cold / breezy area. Let the bird dry out or, to help things along, get a hair dryer set on low breeze, low heat. Many keets love this part, just try to blow dry the keet from a distance so you do not blast the poor little thing with air!

Sleep

Parakeets need to sleep 10-12 hours every day. The vast majority of this is done at night. The cave should be covered with a cloth so it is dark and they feel safe. In nature, parakeets nest in hollows they gnaw out of Eucalyptus trees. You want your cage to sort of resemble that closed-in hollow so they feel safe and protected when they sleep.

Parakeets also take naps during the day when it is quiet. They will often stretch and yawn before falling asleep, or after waking up.

Parakeets will often sleep just by closing their eyes. But they will also perch on one foot sometimes, like a flamingo, to give their other foot a rest for a while.

They also sometimes tuck their heads back on top of their backs, against a wing, to give their neck muscles a rest.

Stretching

Pretty much every animal stretches. Dogs stretch. Cats stretch. Humans stretch. A stretch is how an animal relaxes its muscles. Stretching is what we do when we wake up in the morning, and it's often what we do before we snuggle down for a nap or sleep.

Parakeets need to sleep 8-10 hours every night in a quiet, dark, sheltered location. Parakeets also take naps

Lisa Shea

during the day when it is quiet. They will often stretch and yawn before falling asleep, or after waking up.

One Foot

Parakeets don't lie down on their sides. Their poor feet must support their bodies 24 hours a day, 7 days a week, 365 days a year. Just imagine if you had to stand up on your feet for your entire life! Your feet would get VERY tired and want to have a rest.

Santo does a one-foot

To help their feet get a momentary rest, parakeets will perch on one foot sometimes. You've probably seen flamingos do this in movies. This lets the parakeet give their lifted foot a rest for a while.

Santo again does a one-foot

This is VERY normal behavior. Do try to make sure
that the keet is using different feet every once in a while
though. If your keet always hops around on one foot
only, and will not put weight on the second foot, it's a
sign that something is wrong with that second foot and
that the keet needs to be taken quickly to a vet.

Parakeets aren't perfectly still when they one-foot.
They are constantly adjusting their balance. Try standing
on one foot yourself for a minute. Really, stand up and
give it a try :) You'll find that you wiggle a little left and
right, maintaining your balance.

Head Tuck

When humans, dogs and cats sleep, they get to put their head down to rest their neck muscles. Parakeets don't lie on the ground, so they have to hold their head up all the time. Think of how tired your neck would be if you never got to rest your head on a pillow! Parakeets need to occasionally rest their neck muscles, too. This is why they do the "head tuck" sometimes.

Pinto does the head tuck

This is sometimes, incorrectly, called "tucking their head under their wing". A bird doesn't stuff its head under its wing :). Really it is nuzzling its head into its soft back feathers, like a built-in pillow. This lets them rest their head, and also if it's bright out, it gives them some shelter from the sun. It's like you pulling down the shades to make it darker. All animals find it easier to sleep when it's dark, vs when it's light out.

Ivory head tucks

Nazo head tucks

Wild Birds and Mirrors

Parakeets are flock birds, used to living in giant flocks. So it's no surprise that if you have a single, lonely budgie and there are chickadees or other birds outside your window, your budgie will long to be with them. Your budgie might spend all its time pining after those feathered friends, and ignore you. Birds long to be with other birds. When they are alone it makes them feel like they're in danger.

If you want to teach your parakeet how to talk, you want to start with a single, male, very young parakeet. But it is critical that you spend enough time with your parakeet so the parakeet thinks of YOU as his flockmate, that he is not alone and lonely. You need to be around him a lot so he learns to want to be with you, to want to talk like you and talk TO you.

If you give your bird playmates of any birding kind - either another parakeet, a mirror, or access to a window full of outside birds, your bird is going to gravitate towards them and not pay as much attention to you. After all, how could YOU be a flockmate when he sees other, much more birdlike creatures nearby?

Therefore, if your aim is to really train the bird and have it talk and be a member of the family, you have to hold off on any other bird substitutes. Don't get a second bird, hide all mirrors, keep the outside bird visibility to a minimum. You want your parakeet to think of YOU as his flock, to want to talk to you.

After 6 months or so, your bird should have begun to talk and fully adopted you as a flockmate. At this point you can start introducing other birds and not worry about it as much. Especially if you're not home all the time, it would be kind to your bird to give him some companionship for when you can't be there. You don't want your bird pining of loneliness for hours and hours while you're at work or school! The tradeoff might be that the parakeet talks less and fweeps more, but there always has to be a balance in life. The most important thing is for your parakeet to lead a happy, stress-free life. It's up to you if that means you can be there to keep the parakeet company, or if you get a companion for your parakeet once its basic training is done.

Traveling and Vacation

There are many situations that will require a parakeet to travel with you. It could be that you're moving to a new house or apartment. Maybe you have a summer home you go to for many months. Parakeets travel each time they go to the vet's office. Here is advice on the variety of situations you might face.

To Take or Not Take the Keet
Of course, some situations require the keet to travel, if the whole family is moving or if the keet is going to a vet. But if you're just going away for a few days, it's wiser to leave the keet at home. Moving in a car or other vehicle in a cage is inherently dangerous for a keet - sudden stops or turns can throw them within their cage. There are no parakeet seatbelts, even if you do seatbelt the whole cage to the seat. Keets can stay home alone for up to a week as long as you fill their cage up with seed and water, and play some soft music for them to listen to. It's better all around, during the short trips, that the keet just stay put and is comfortable.

Travel by Car
You need to have a small, travel cage for your keet - not the large one that has lots of "projectile" room within it. You don't want ANY toys in the cage that might swing and hurt the keet. No swings, either. This travel cage should be as small as possible with one perch to sit on, and a small holder for food and water. That lets the keet stay fed, but minimizes the chances of injury.

Have a towel to put over the cage to keep out drafts and hot sun depending on the time of year. Make sure you pre-warm or pre-cool the car to a reasonable temperature before the keet is moved into it, and go quickly through the ambient outside air if it's not a gentle temperature.

I highly recommend twist-tying shut the door of the cage, just in case. The last thing you want to happen is have your keet escape while you're moving from one place to another. It's hard enough for a keet to find their way home when they escape FROM home.

Try to seatbelt the cage into place as much as possible. Sure, it's nice to think you will hold the cage - but believe me, in an accident you can't control what your arms do. You want the keet's cage to be as secure as possible so it does not become a flying projectile - injuring the keet and others.

Even if you're stressed out, try to keep things quiet and calm. Your stress will agitate the keet and make her really nervous about what is going on. She looks to you for guidance and stability. Talk to her in quiet, even tones and let her know everything will be OK soon. Keets are very smart and learn to settle in to new locations very quickly, as long as they are reassured by their "flockmates" (i.e. you) that everything is OK.

Travel by Train / Bus
Many of the same guidelines apply for train and bus travel. Ask in advance with the transit company if there are any rules regarding parakeets. Most will say that the keet is fine as long as they stay on your lap. Unfortunately most busses and trains do not have seatbelts, but you just do the best you can.

Travel by Airplane

You will usually need to go to your vet in advance of the trip and get a health certificate, saying the bird is fully checked up and healthy. Then you'll need to pay a fee to the airline for the pet transfer. Again, make sure there is just a small cage with nothing in it but food and water, and check on the water every once in a while to make sure it hasn't all spilled out.

An Older Parakeet

A well cared for parakeet can easily live to be 10 to 15 years old. Some even live to the age of 20! So it's no surprise, with 8 million parakeet owners in the US (and many more millions around the world) that some percentage of them are caring for older parakeets. It may be that your beloved pet has stayed with you for many years, or it might be that you've adopted an older parakeet from another person.

If you're adopting an older bird, read through all the suggestions of Caring for a New Bird. Most of the same things will apply to you. Your bird will be nervous, afraid, and cautious. Imagine what it would be like if you suddenly moved from your comfort- able house halfway around the world, to a new land, a brand new house, people who spoke a new language, a new culture, new foods. You would be nervous and scared too! Your parakeet needs time to adjust to his new surroundings, to get used to the people and smells and sounds around him.

Give him time to adjust. Let him learn that his new cage is safe, his new corner of the world is a nice one. That he will be fed regularly and his water is fresh. After a week or two, he will begin to relax and accept this new home as a nice one. Then when you start on finger training, he will be open to accepting your hand as a friendly part of his new world.

Health of an Older Bird

A bird that has made it past age seven is probably not going to develop tumors, which is the main form of sickness to hit parakeets. So in a way, an older bird has already proven that it's healthy! Parakeets don't really slow down and need nursing care. Birds like that in the wild tend to get eaten quickly. So if anything, a parakeet tends to be lively and robust pretty much until the day that he passes on.

Be sure to keep fresh food in his cage daily, and change the water daily too. Since there probably won't be obvious signs that something is really going wrong with him, keep an eye on the more subtle changes. Is his poop suddenly very watery? Is he refusing to eat foods he normally loves? Is he having trouble balancing on his perch? All of these might be signs to take him to the vet and see if something can be done.

Above all else, be sure to keep interacting with your bird and making him feel loved and cared for. A budgie's primary concern is that he is a part of his flock, and that he is accepted by his flock. Let him know that he is thought of daily, that you are there for him, and that he is loved. Parakeets are VERY social and your presence there will be a warm comfort as he ages.

Multiple Parakeets

Birds naturally live in flocks. Especially parakeets. Back in Australia where they hang out in the wild, there are HUGE flocks of parakeets that, only a century or two ago, would darken the sky and look like a cloud when they flew overhead. They're simply not meant to live alone.

True, if you want to teach your parakeet how to talk, you want to start with a single, male, very young parakeet. The parakeet has to think of YOU as its flock, and want to talk the way you do. However, once you get it talking (or give up after 8 or 12 months), it's time to get your bird a companion. To leave your parakeet alone is extremely cruel, and some birds even go insane if they're abandoned like this.

The first step is to get another young bird. Make sure it's got stripes on its forehead, and that it's as young as possible. You want it to be able to adjust easily to your current bird. Next, get a little cage for it, so it can have its own spot while the two birds get used to each other. It can be an inexpensive $10 one - just somewhere for it to have as its own. Keep the cages close, but keep the birds separate. You want the birds to learn to trust each other without feeling territorial.

Once they're relatively friendly, open both cages (with the doors and windows closed of course!) and let the birds get to know each other. With their own cage to retreat to for safety, they should get to become friends.

Now start letting both of them share the bigger cage. Make sure you have 2 of every- thing - 2 food dishes, 2 water dishes, 2 cuttlebones. You don't want them to have to fight for who gets to eat! The more they feel that they're both being taken care of, the happier they both will be. And, once they're content living together, they'll be a 'flock' and will be happy!

Note that I've read some nonsense on other websites about how multiple parakeets MUST all be male. This is NOT true. I have had male parakeets, female parakeets, and mixed groups. My current three parakeets are all female. They are QUITE happy together and preen each other! If you raise your parakeets in a stress-free, happy environment where there's enough food and bathtubs for all, they will get along fine.

Social Life

We've covered why parakeets should live in groups. They are trained by nature to live in giant flocks of hundreds or thousands of birds for safety and protection. For a parakeet, to be all alone is a sign of danger and one that makes them feel threatened. But what happens if you put two or more parakeets together?

First off, parakeets are like all other living creatures. They have moods. Sometimes they'll be happy with each other. Sometimes they'll be cranky. You have to accept the ups and downs. You can't really "interfere" in parakeet squabbles. Birds develop a "pecking order" where the dominant bird gets things first and shows who is boss. The other birds learn to accept this and they develop a happy world.

It's VERY important that you make their life as stress-free as possible. They should get fresh food daily, with separate food cups for each bird spaced apart from each other. There should be fresh water daily. Treats should be given in multiples so each bird has his or her own. If you have 3 birds, get 3 bathtubs. The less your birds have to fight over necessities of life, the more happy they will be together.

Courtship

Courtship isn't necessarily just about male-female. It can be male-male or female-female. It simply means "I love you, fellow feathered creature"! Birds can even court their human owners. Parakeets don't have presents like rings or flowers to bring their loved ones. So they bring them food. Parakeets don't have hands, so they eat the seed, carry it in their stomach to their partner, regurgitate it back up, and then pass it mouth to mouth to their partner.

This is what we humans THINK is kissing. It's not kissing! It's the partner sharing regurgitated food or making the motions. This is also how mommy birds care for their babies, so in either case it's the ultimate sign of tenderness.

Preening

Birds don't have hands to itch themselves with - they can only use their feet and beak. There are some hard to get spots on a parakeet's body! They will sometimes preen each other, getting to those itchy spots and helping to keep the feathers clean.

Make sure that the birds are preening gently and not actively yanking to annoy. Usually the active yanking of feathers is accompanied by the "ACK! ACK! ACK!" annoyance of the *yankee*.

Chasing

I see this all the time with my three parakeets. Pinto will be sitting to one side. Nazo will side step down the perch until she's next to Pinto. But Pinto wanted to be alone. So Pinto flies off to another perch. Nazo goes right after her and side-steps along to be near her.

It's like real life. Sometimes you want to be alone. Sometimes you want to be with some- one. The needs don't always match up well. Eventually the birds will find a compromise.

Biting / Pecking

It's hard to tell when parakeet behavior crosses from just "leave me alone" snaps to full blown harassment. If you have a generally happy cage, with plenty of food, water, good temperature, baths and playtime, and music playing, it's hard to imagine that one parakeet would get so truly angry that he would start harassing another bird. They are too good natured for that. Sure, they'll bite at each other when they're grumpy, or when they want to be left alone. But that should be an occasional thing.

But sometimes you just get a bird with a bad attitude. Maybe this bird was left alone for years and years in a dark corner and became a brooding grump. Now you get yourself a cute little baby and pop it in the same cage, and the brooding grump is furious. In this kind of a situation I *highly* recommend getting two separate cages, side by side, and letting the grump have his own space. Maybe over time he will come to accept the new- comer - but old dogs learn tricks rather slowly. A bird that's become territorial and angry and defensive will take many months to outgrow that behavior.

Parakeet Breeding

You love parakeets - and the idea of making millions of your own parakeets is some- what alluring. Just what should you consider before you get into breeding parakeets?

First off, of course, the parakeets both have to be adults. Young parakeets have little interest in sex :) Parakeets become adults at around 6 months, but I would highly recommend waiting until the keets were a year or older. Parakeets take this long to learn to talk and to fully become part of a household. It seems awfully cruel to me to force a barely- born creature to go through the stresses of childbirth when it has barely become settled in its world. If your only aim was to breed thousands of budgies, I suppose 6 months is where you would begin. But if these birds are your pets, I would wait.

Next, of course, they have to be male and female. While you might THINK they are, unless you are really certain, you could easily have 2 males or 2 females. They of course would lack the appropriate parts to connect together to make fertilized eggs with. You can't tell just by courtship behavior. Females will court females, males will court males. It shows that they care for each other. But only a male parakeet plus a parakeet equals fertilized eggs. Note that females WILL lay eggs even if a male isn't around - they just won't turn into parakeet babies. It's like with chickens. Chickens lay eggs all the time that are unfertilized, these are what we eat for breakfast.

OK, assuming you did have one male, one female,

239

both adults, the parakeets might just not be interested in sex with each other. There are all sorts of reasons why. Parakeets are extremely intelligent and don't just mate with any random parakeet. So there is never a guarantee that a pair of keets will start creating babies. You need to be happy with them as pets and not think of them as baby producers.

If you're interested in the physical aspect of bird mating, then yes, a male bird has a sex organ, just like male humans do. He is called the "cock". The female bird has an opening between her legs, just like female humans do. She is the "hen". Just like with dogs, cats, horses and other creatures, the male gets behind the female and puts his organ inside her from behind. This is even a common style of sex for humans, too. In any case, when this happens, the female's eggs are then fertilized and able to make baby parakeets. If she lays eggs without having this interaction with a male, the eggs are unfertilized.

That's like most chickens that lay eggs for us humans to eat. Those eggs you get in the supermarket are unfertilized eggs. They won't turn into baby chickens.

I personally feel strongly that a person really should own parakeets for several years before they start thinking about raising baby parakeets. It is a serious thing, to cause new life to be brought in this world and be dependent on you. ALL sorts of problems can happen during childbirth. Heck even with human beings, I believe I was just reading that one out of 5 women *DIE* in Iraq while trying to have a baby. Those are real life human females who are pregnant in the year 2004, who are dying because of lack of proper care.

Parakeet parents can get egg bound and can have other things happen to them during the stresses of childbirth. The human owner would need to be able to help them through the process so they did not die. Baby parakeets are of course very tiny and can need medicine and other care.

Many breeders go through special training programs before they start raising young birds. Some even get college degrees in animal care. If you are going to take that step and start encouraging your birds to go through the stress of childbirth you need to at least have a book or two on the topic - and I highly suggest you go talk to a bird breeder in your area to find out what you are getting yourself into. You can't just wave goodbye to them in the morning and go to school all day. You have to be there to care for the chicks.

Also be sure you get in contact with a bird veterinarian in your area and have the vet check out both parents to make sure they are healthy enough to breed. That way the vet also knows who you are so if you call her up in the middle of the night with an emergency, she'll meet you at the office to take care of it.

Once you've done those things, good luck with your breeding adventures!

Other Pets

If you've got a parakeet in the house, you might also have cats and dogs as well. Be sure to read these pages to learn how to ensure your pets stay healthy and happy!

Cats/ Cat Saliva

Anyone who has seen Sylvester and Tweety cartoons knows that it is in a cat's nature to want to catch and eat small creatures like birds and mice. Most bird feeder owners have watched a neighborhood cat stalk around the edges of the area, eyes intent on the birds, waiting for their chance to pounce. It is not wrong of the cat, or bad, or inappropriate. This is what cats are born to do. This is how a cat survives and thrives in the wild. Cats are made to eat birds.

I have owned parakeets all my life, and I have also owned cats all my life. It is certainly very possible for budgies and cats to live together in harmony in a house! The key, as with much else in life, is to be a careful, attentive pet parent.

Yes, it might be that for five years your bird has been completely safe with your cat. However, every living creature has its temperamental moments. Maybe the cat is annoyed because his tummy is upset, and he's exceptionally cranky. The bird happens to land near his paw, and he swats at the bird more out of temporary annoyance than anything else. The one swipe can kill.

New pet owners might think it's "cute" to have their cats near their birds - gazing in the cage, only inches away. Remember that for the cat, their instincts tell them to eat feathered little creatures. This is honing their knowledge of the bird, for potential use later on. For the birds, every instinct in a bird's body is to FLEE FLEE FLEE from this very dangerous predator. The way birds stay alive is to get away from cats! Even if your bird seems calm, it may be staying as still as possible until the predator leaves. The extra stress on the bird's lungs and heart can cause serious medical issues.

Keep the cage up high enough that the cat cannot jump to it. Keep in mind that many cats can leap almost to door height! Look on YouTube for the videos if you doubt a cat's amazing jumping skills. Don't think that a cat in a cage is safe. When I was eight, my cage setup in my room was that the cage was suspended from a pole in the center of the room. It was one of those poles that went up, curved around the cage, and then had a hook. So the cage was at higher-than-my-shoulders height (for an eight year old) that I had to reach up to - and it was in the very center of the room. The cat still managed to leap up onto the cage and pull the parakeet THROUGH the thin bars to eat it. You can't blame the cat. Eating birds is what cats do. You can't blame the keet - it was helpless! It is the responsibility of the keet parents to ensure the keet is safe from harm.

Cat Saliva and Parakeets

You'll find many web pages out there perpetuating the idea that all cat saliva is somehow toxic to all parakeets. This is NOT true. Rather, cat saliva (and dog saliva) can sometimes have bacteria in them. Just like dirt can have bacteria in it, and the basement floor can have bacteria in it, and so on. However, you don't tend to get dirt of basement floor grit all over your parakeet! However, if you somehow managed to let your cat lick your parakeet, now that bacteria set is on your parakeet - and the parakeet's sensitive system can quickly be overwhelmed by it.

It's not just parakeets that are affected by this type

of bacteria. If you had an open wound - let's say a paper cut on your finger - and you let your cat lick the wound, now that bacteria is coursing through your system. There are a number of reports of people getting fairly seriously sick as a result. There's a reason you put band-aids on wounds - to keep out dirt and bacteria.

An additional reason that people sometimes believe the "all cat saliva is toxic" myth is that cat teeth and cat claws make deep, thin holes in the body. These are puncture wounds. Those teeth and claws - as mentioned - have bacteria on them. So it is like the cat is taking a needle and injecting bacteria deep into your system. Your normal cleaning things you do for wounds - washing them with soap, etc. - doesn't get that bacteria out. So it's far more likely to fester and cause problems, compared with say a paper cut. This is the same sort of reason that nail puncture wounds are so dangerous. Anything that makes a deep but narrow hole into your body is hard to clean properly.

Cats clean themselves by licking their entire bodies - repeatedly. So a cat's entire body is coated with saliva. Make sure, before you take your parakeet out to play with her, that you wash your hands well. You don't want to pet your cat, have your hands coated with cat saliva and bacteria, and then go transfer all of those items onto your parakeet's body.

So what's the take home lesson? First, keep your keets safe and away from your cats except when you are physically there in the room. Even if you're there, don't let your parakeet out when the cat is around. Second, make sure you always wash your hands before you interact with your parakeet, so you do not accidentally transfer any bacteria on her.

In the situation where your parakeet accidentally gets either touched by the cat or touched by you after you've played with the cat, I highly suggest getting a fresh bathtub quickly into the keet's area and trying to encourage her to wash. Also, keep an eye on your keet for any sign of illness. It's likely your keet will be fine - after all, not every cat has a dangerous bacteria in it - but it's always best to be safe!

Lisa Shea

Dogs/ Dog Saliva

When I was growing up we had a cockapoo - a black, curly haired dog named O'Henry. We have always had parakeets, so there were many instances when O'Henry and our parakeets were in the same room. We never had an issue with our dog showing an interest in our budgies.

However, here is a cautionary tale. A friend of mine had a dog who was also very peaceful and calm, who adored kittens and all creatures large and small. My friend and his dog went to visit Joe who had a well-trained parrot. They were all sitting in the living room, smiling and laughing. The dog was peacefully resting at my friend's feet.

The parrot's owner put out his arm, and called to his parrot to fly down to him. The parrot put out his wings and gracefully soared across the room towards the arm.

The dog jumped into the air, grabbed the parrot, gave it a quick shake to break his neck, and then lay down again. The entire event took maybe a second at the most.

Dogs eat birds. It is what they have been trained by nature for tens of thousands of years to do. It is not bad, or wrong, or evil of them to eat birds. It is part of being a dog. As much as you might try to train a dog not to eat a bird, there is always going to be a part of a dog's mind which says BIRD = FOOD. Even if your dog is quiet and peaceful, he still eats food! He does not think of eating a bird as a violent thing. He simply sees it as an eating task, just like he eats food out of a bowl. If the mood strikes him, he'll eat.

It's also important to keep in mind that every living creature has its temperamental moments. Let's say your dog's paw is hurting because a stone is stuck in it. So he's grumpy. The parakeet gets near him and he swats his paw, just to get the annoying little thing out of his way. The parakeet is now dead, and the dog's being yelled at, and the dog has no idea why.

The parakeet owner needs to take the responsibility to be the responsible parent. The dog should not be around the parakeet when it is out of the cage. Even when the parakeet is in the cage, the cage should be high enough that the dog can't easily get to it or knock it over. Remember, it's not that the dog is being "mean" by eating the parakeet. He is simply hungry, or curious, or both.

It's also important that the cage be away from the dog for the parakeet's sanity. Remember that little birds survive in the wild because they are deathly afraid of predators and flee at even the slightest sign that a predator is nearby. The slow parakeets are the dead parakeets. If a parakeet sees a predator's eyes watching them, it upsets them greatly. Sometimes they flap around like crazy. Sometimes they sit still hoping maybe the predator will go away. It's never good for a parakeet's health to have a predator's eyes watching it.

Dog Saliva and Parakeets

Sometimes you read on various websites that dog saliva is toxic to birds. That is not true! You also read that dog saliva is some sort of a miracle substance that helps wounds to heal. The truth is somewhere in the middle. A dog's tongue (just like a cat's tongue) can have a variety of bacteria on it. These bacteria can be harmful. There are a number of cases of a dog licking a human and getting that saliva into an open wound, like a paper cut, and causing serious harm. The issue isn't one of the dog in particular. It's more that the person would not put dirt or dust into an open wound - but they are willing to let the dog lick the wound.

With parakeets, they have tiny bodies which are sensitive to bacteria. You probably don't let your parakeet play in the dirt or crawl around on your grubby basement floor. But if you let dog saliva get onto your parakeet, that's in essence what you've done. That bacteria swarm can now affect the parakeet.

As you might imagine, the same holds true if you pet your dog - since dogs lick themselves and get their saliva on their fur - and then pet your parakeet. Your hand is now transferring that bacteria swarm from your dog onto your parakeet.

So the key is of course not to let your dog lick your parakeet, and to wash your own hands before you play with your parakeet. That way you don't become a bacteria carrier.

If your dog does happen to lick your parakeet through a dangerous accident, then I would get a fresh bathtub of water for your keet and encourage her to wash off as much as possible. That way you get the bacteria off of her. Then be sure to watch her for signs of illness. It's not as if your keet was just coated in arsenic - but you want to be as safe as possible!

Toys and Fun

One of the most important things you can have in a parakeet cage, besides food and water, is a toy or two. A parakeet is a VERY intelligent creature and can literally go stir crazy if he doesn't have something to play with.

Also, a parakeet needs new toys (or at least a rotation of toys) every few months. They will get incredibly bored if they have to look at the exact same toy every day. I try to rotate the toys in my parakeets' cage every month or so.

Parakeets love sound, so one of the best kinds of toys to get for a parakeet is one with a bell. Do NOT get the jingle-bell type of bell that is a metal sphere with little holes cut in it. A parakeet's toes can easily get stuck in those little holes.

Above is an example of two GOOD bell toys.

The one on the left is a rope-and-wood bell. The keets love chewing on the wood bits and can even hang on the rope. The one on the right is plastic - it lasts longer and the keets love the bright colors. Getting different types of toys of different materials helps keep your keets entertained.

Another very popular keet toy is a series of rings. We have both rope rings and plastic rings. The rings are big enough for the keets to climb through, which they love to do. They are quite the acrobats! Here is a picture of a rope ring set.

Be sure to treat any parakeet toy just like you
would a toy for an infant. Make sure there are no sharp
edges and that it cannot break easily. Make sure there are
no tiny parts that might fall off and get eaten by
accident. Don't leave any long strings lying around.

Parakeets can sometimes get themselves tangled up in rope or thread that is loose.

DO expect your parakeets to gnaw any toy part that's gnawable. That's what parakeets do! You should always have at least one wood-based toy in the cage, and expect to replace that one regularly :)

Almond Hanging Toy

Parakeets love nuts, and almonds are quite good for them. Almonds are good for YOU too so be sure to eat some while you put together this toy!

Get a small needle and a length of string. Tie the end of the string to a wooden bead or other parakeet-safe object to keep the almonds from sliding off the string. Now push the needle gently into the first almond. Having a thimble is really helpful here because it'll take some force to get the needle into the almond. Put the almond on something safe - like a pad of paper - when you do this, so the needle poking out the other side doesn't poke into anything bad.

Once the needle is starting to poke out the other side of the almond, turn the almond over. Press the almond down onto the needle, again pressing down against a pad of paper or something else safe to dent.

When you get the needle all the way into the almond, i.e. when the head of the needle is now flush with the almond's outer edge, it's time to "pull" the needle the rest of the way through. I found a pair of nail clippers was perfect for this. They would grab tightly onto the needle and allow you to pull it through. If you have a pair of jewelry clamps those would also work well.

Continue on with another 10-15 almonds, making a chain. This is great for parakeets because not only can they play with it, but they can eat it too!

Cheerio Hanging Toy

Cheerios are a great parakeet snack. Be sure NOT to get froot loops or other artificially colored treats! The last thing a parakeet needs is exceed sugar and chemicals in his or her body. Remember, they have tiny bodies! Even small doses of chemicals can have a serious effect on them.

Take some twine or cotton thread and string the cheerios on it. You can tie the string around one of the cheerios for the bottom, so the rest don't all fall off. You can also tie the string sideways in the cage, so the parakeet can slide the cheerios back and forth on the string. Be sure not to leave excess string lying around, otherwise the para- keet might get wrapped up in it and choke.

Peanut Butter Ring Toy

The big warning here is do NOT use cardboard tubes from toilet paper!! Parakeets love to chew and any cardboard you put near them is going to be gnawed on. You do NOT want them gnawing on something that has been handled by unclean hands often. Be sure to get cardboard tubes from paper towel rolls and other sources.

Take a paper towel tube and cut 1/4" rings from it. Four or five are a good number to work with. Take hemp twine or cotton thread and connect the rings to each other so you form a long chain. Now smear peanut butter onto each ring and roll it in seeds.

Hang in the cage - the parakeets will love gnawing on the wrings, eating the food and climbing through them!

Popcorn String Toy

Most of us remember making popcorn strings to put on trees at Christmas! This is a great treat for all birds - wild birds outside, and tame birds inside.

Simply pop up a batch of popcorn. It's best to use unbuttered popcorn since most of the "buttered" varieties are made with fake butter and chemicals. Now thread a needle and put a bead or something parakeet-safe at the end so the popcorn doesn't just slide off.

Start threading the popcorn on the thread! Compared to other things you can thread for birds to eat, popcorn is VERY easy to do. When you're done, tie off the other end, and hang it up! For birds outside, you can do very long chains to drape on the trees in your yard. For your parakeets inside, just 10 or 15 popcorns will do the trick nicely.

They'll love the chewing!

Egg Carton Surprise Toy

Parakeets LOVE to chew things, and they love fun discoveries. This toy combines the two!

Break off four cubes of a cardboard egg carton, both the top and bottom together. Put a variety of treats into the cubes - parakeet safe toys, seeds, nuts, veggies, etc. Now close the cubes and put them into the cage.

I have a circular parakeet bathtub that I have mounted on the inside of the cage - it works great to put the cubes into this (empty) bathtub so they can play with it up high and not get it all dirty from the bottom of their cage. You can put it on top of their cage for their 'out of cage' playtime, put it in their play gym, or wherever else works well for you.

The parakeets LOVE to chew so they will enjoy chewing on their toy - and will be thrilled to discover the treats inside!

Cardboard Tube Toy

The big warning here is do NOT use cardboard tubes from toilet paper!! Parakeets love to chew and any cardboard you put near them is going to be gnawed on. You do NOT want them gnawing on something that has been handled by unclean hands often. Be sure to get cardboard tubes from paper towel rolls and other sources.

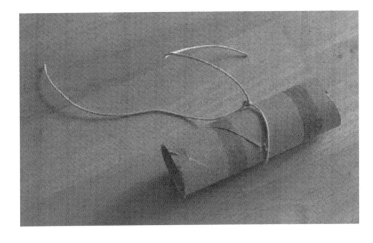

Cut a paper towel roll tube in half. Cut two small holes on either side of the top center. Run a good thickness string through there - I like hemp, but you can use cotton as well. Run the thread through the 2 holes so that the cardboard can't "slip out" from the hangar you are making. I know it's hard to see in this photo, but the string is going IN to the tube at the

center-point of the tube, on the top of the picture
underneath the knot. The string comes back out of the
tube out of another hole lower down on the forward
side.

Wrap the string around the bottom of the tube,
then up again and tie it in a knot. This stops the tube
from easily flopping back and forth like a see-saw.
Now tie this tube to your cage.

Parakeets are natural acrobats and love climbing in
and around things! Your parakeet should have great fun
climbing in and out of the tube, and chewing on it.
When the parakeet has chewed the tube up completely,
put in a new one!

Building a Bird Play-gym

Parakeets and other birds are incredibly intelligent. Just imagine if you were stuck in the exact same single room for 10 solid years, without anything in it changing, without ever going out of that room, with nothing new to look at? That's what it's like for a parakeet! So it's important to give them new toys occasionally, play different kinds of music for them, let them look out a window, and especially give them a play gym.

A play gym lets your parakeet have fun, swing around, gnaw on things, and stretch its wings. Parakeets are incredibly acrobatic and love to play. Start out by reading about safe parakeet toys. Once you have a few toys in your parakeet's cage and are rotating them regularly, it might be time to look into building a fun play-gym for your parakeets. It's pretty easy to do, and can give them hours of fun each day!

We built this gym for our 3 parakeets and keep it right next to the cage. That way when they're out (always with supervision!) they can easily hop over to the gym and play on it. When they are sleepy or hungry, they head right back to their cage to rest up.

The wood must be untreated and natural. You don't want any nasty preservatives in something the parakeets will chew! And yes they WILL chew your gym. That's what parakeets do! Their natural behavior in the wild is to chew holes in Eucalyptus trees to make their nests. So they like to chew. It also keeps their beaks trimmed.

Use wood that they can gnaw. Keets love to gnaw, and it keeps their beak trimmed.

Make perches of different sizes, to help their feet stay supple.

Let the toys be attached and detached easily so you can swap toys occasionally.

Provide a ledge for a bathtub, so they can have fun splashing.

Put the gym somewhere stable but relatively high. Keets like to be high up, it lets them feel safe.

Definitely no sharp edges!! Attach the wood with glue where you can, NON TOXIC GLUE.

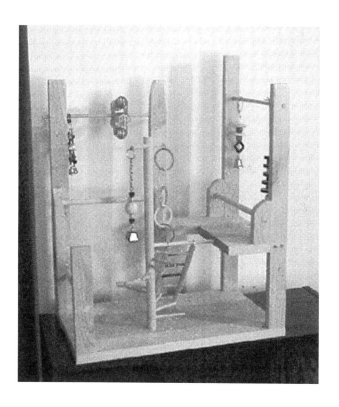

Fun Parakeet Thoughts

Parakeets are some of the most popular pets in the world. Here are a variety of fun facts and thoughts about your little parakeet friends!

Lisa Shea

Fluorescent Budgie Feathers

First off, parakeets do *NOT GLOW IN THE DARK*! To think that these poor little birds would turn into giant night-lights after dark would be silly! Just think of all those predators out roaming the night saying "Jeez, where do I find a tasty meal?" The predators would look up in the trees and see bunches of glowing little parakeets, and have a buffet.

The research done in the science journal called *Nature* by Katherine Arnold involved the breeding feathers of budgies - the ones around their head and neck. When budgies are out in the sun all day, those feathers absorb ultraviolet light from the sun - just like a blacktop of a driveway would absorb the sun's warmth and get warm. After dark, just as the driveway stays warm for a while and radiates that heat, the bird's feathers give off a fluorescent glow. You can see that if you have a fluorescent light. But of course your budgie would have had to have been in the sun for a few hours first!

Why do the bird's breeding feathers fluoresce? It's a sign of a healthy bird, that they have enough breeding feathers to absorb the ultraviolet rays, and also a sign of a healthy bird that they were out in the sun for a long while. Parakeets need lots of sunlight to absorb the vitamins from it.

Ms. Arnold's research therefore was to put sunblock on a bunch of parakeets, so their feathers did

NOT fluoresce. She found that parakeets of the opposite sex - potential mates - began ignoring the birds that had been sun-blocked! So parakeets use that glow to help them determine which birds are suitable for dating. Other birds of the same sex stayed friendly, so it wasn't a "you are a bad parakeet" thing. It was a "you are not a suitable partner to raise kids with" thing.

How do parakeets see this fluorescence? Obviously they don't have fluorescent lights out on the Australian plains of their homelands!! All advanced eyes have rods and cones in them that detect light and shapes and turn those into vision for our brains.

While human eyes don't have cones that reach into the fluorescent spectrum, parakeet eyes do have double cones that can see those wavelengths. So when a parakeet looks at another parakeet, that glow is one of the things they can see!

Yellow Parakeet Cocktail Recipe

If you're of legal drinking age, here is a traditional cocktail that you can toast your parakeet with!

Ingredients:
2 oz Orange juice
1 oz Pineapple juice
1 oz Midori
1/2 oz Bacardi
1/2 oz Banana
1 splash Sour mix

Fill a glass with ice and add the ingredients in order. Enjoy!

Parakeets and Budgies in Movies

Parakeets are such wonderful pets - it's no wonder that they are featured in many movies! Here are some great movies to watch with your parakeet by your side.

I Robot with Will Smith
Dumb and Dumber
Time of the Wolf
A Nightmare On Elm Street Part 2
Teacher's Pet
Stuart Little 2
The Thin Red Line
A Woman's Tale
Bride of the Monster

Movies that do NOT have parakeets but are sometimes mistakenly credited with them are:

The Golden Child - this was a green parrot.

Nazo and the Pizza Slice

Nazo is a very adventurous parakeet. She loves trying new foods, while my other two parakeets hide in the corner terrified of the "scary piece of celery." The key for Nazo is if HUMANS think it is food. If she sees one of us humans eating something, Nazo wants to try it, too.

One day we had Nazo's cage in the kitchen and had brought home a box of pepperoni pizza. We opened Nazo's cage door so she could hang out with us while we ate dinner. Nazo watched us with great interest as we consumed our pizza slices.

Near the end of the meal, my son, James, reached for a final slice and brought it up to his mouth. Nazo saw her chance! She flew down from the cage, landed RIGHT in the middle of the slice of pizza (cheese, sauce, and all) and began eating the crust from between James' fingers! Her tail was sticking right in James' face.

We thought this was hilariously funny and James put the slice down so Nazo could eat it in peace. She pecked away with great glee, nibbling the crust and the tomato bits. We got some paper towels and when she was done we convinced her to hop around on the paper towel for a while, so her feet would get cleaned off.

We're careful not to let her out when we eat pizza, now, in case a piece is still hot enough to hurt her! But we do save the crusts for her, which she enjoys greatly :).

Summary

Parakeets can live just as long as most cats and dogs, are incredibly intelligent, can learn to talk, and cost very little compared to most other pets. They can be kept in apartments, dorm rooms, and other small locations with little difficulty. They are loyal, friendly and very cute!

I hope this book has helped you to better care for your keet, and to build the bonds of love and friendship.

Enjoy!

Parakeets

Thank you for reading this Parakeets and Budgies book! I hope you found some new tips to help you raise happy, healthy pets

If you enjoyed this book, please leave feedback on Amazon, Goodreads, and any other systems you use. Together we can help make a difference!

If you have a tip I didn't cover, please let me know! Together we can help each other achieve our dreams.

All author's proceeds benefit charity.

Be sure to sign up for my free newsletter! You'll get alerts of free books, discounts, and new releases. I run my own newsletter server – nobody else will ever see your email address. I promise!

http://www.lisashea.com/lisabase/subscribe.html

Dedication

To the Boston Writer's Group, who supports me in all my projects.

To my boyfriend, who encourages me in all of my dreams.

About the Author

Lisa's parents had parakeets before she was born. For most of the past four decades she has raised parakeets, enjoying their friendly presence, singing to them, playing with them, and making treats for them.

Lisa runs a parakeet-focused forum at LisaShea.com

Please visit the following pages for news about free books, discounted releases, and new launches. Feel free to post questions there – I strive to answer within a day!

Facebook:
https://www.facebook.com/LisaSheaAuthor

Twitter:
https://twitter.com/LisaSheaAuthor

Google+:
https://plus.google.com/+LisaSheaAuthor/posts

Blog:
http://www.lisashea.com/lisabase/blog/

Newsletter:
http://www.lisashea.com/lisabase/subscribe.html

Share the news – we all want to enjoy interesting novels!

Parakeets

Medieval romance novels:
Seeking the Truth
Knowing Yourself
A Sense of Duty
Creating Memories
Looking Back
Badge of Honor
Lady in Red
Finding Peace
Believing your Eyes
Trusting in Faith
Sworn Loyalty
In A Glance

Each medieval novel is a stand-alone story set in medieval England. The novels can be read in any order and have entirely separate casts of characters. In comparison, the below series are each linear and connected in nature.

Cozy murder mystery series:
Aspen Allegations | Birch Blackguards | Cedar Conundrums

Sci-fi adventure romance series:
Aquarian Awakenings | Betelgeuse Beguiling | Centauri Chaos | Draconis Discord

Dystopian journey series:
Into the Wasteland | He Who Was Living | Broken Images

Scottish regency time-travel series:
One Scottish Lass | A Time Apart | A Circle in Time

1800s Tennessee black / Native American series:
Across the River

Lisa's short stories:
Chartreuse | The Angst of Change | BAAC | Melting | Armsby

Black Cat short stories:
Lisa's 31-book cozy mini mystery series set in Salem Massachusetts begins with:
The Lucky Cat – Black Cat Vol. 1

Here are a few of Lisa's self-help books:

Secrets to Falling Asleep
Get Better Sleep to Improve Health and Reduce Stress

Dream Symbol Encyclopedia
Interpretation and Meaning of Dream Symbols

Lucid Dreaming Guide
Foster Creativity in a Lucid Dream State

Learning to say NO – and YES! To your Dream
Protect your goals while gently helping others succeed

Reduce Stress Instantly
Practical relaxation tips you can use right now for instant stress relief

Time Management Course
Learn to End Procrastination, Increase Productivity, and Reduce Stress

Simple Ways to Make the World Better for Everyone
Every day we wake up is a day to take a fresh path, to help a friend, and to improve our lives.

Author's proceeds from all these books benefit battered women's shelters.
"Be the change you wish to see in the world."

As a special treat, as a warm thank-you for buying this book and supporting the cause of battered women, here's a sneak peek at the first chapter of *Aspen Allegations*.

Aspen Allegations was awarded a 2013 Gold Medal from the Independent Publisher Book Awards.

Aspen Allegations - Chapter 1

What is life?
It is the flash of a firefly in the night.
It is the breath of a buffalo in the wintertime.
It is the little shadow which runs across the grass
and loses itself in the sunset.
~ Crowfoot, Blackfoot warrior

The woods were lovely, dark, and deep. My footfalls on the thick layer of tawny oak leaves made that distinctive crisp-crunch sound that seemed unique in all of nature. The clouds above were soft grey, cottony, a welcome relief from the torrents of Hurricane Sandy which had deluged the east coast two days earlier. Sutton had been lucky. Plum Island, Massachusetts, a mere ninety minutes northeast, had been nearly blown away by eighty-mile-an-hour winds. Here we had seen only a few downed trees, Whitins Pond once again rising over its banks, and the scattering of power outages which seemed to accompany every weather event.

I breathed in a lungful of the rich autumn air tanged with moss, turkey-tail mushroom, and the redolent muskiness of settling vegetation. Nearly all of the deciduous trees had released their weight for the year, helped along in no small part by the gale-force winds of Tuesday. That left only the pine with its greenery of five-needled bursts and the delicate golden sprawls of witch hazel blossoms scattered along the path.

It was nice to be outdoors. Two days of being cooped up in my house-slash-home-office had left me eager to stretch my legs. The Sutton Forest was far quieter than Purgatory Chasm this time of year, in no small part because hunting season had begun a few weeks earlier. The bow-and-arrow set were out stalking the white-tailed deer, and they had just been joined by those eager for coyote, weasel, and fox. I wore a bright orange sarong draped over my jacket in deference to my desire to make it through the day unperforated.

A golden shaft of sunlight streamed across the path, and I smiled at where it highlighted a scattering of what appeared to be small dusty-russet pumpkins. I stooped to pick one up, nudging its segments apart with a thumbnail. A smooth nut stood out within its center. A hickory, perhaps? I would have to look that up later when I returned home. I had finally indulged myself with a smartphone a few years ago when I turned forty, and while I liked to carry it for safety reasons, I preferred to leave it untouched when breathing in the delights of a beautiful day.

The woods were quiet, and I liked them this way. The Sutton Forest network stretched across the middle of the eight-mile-square town, but it seemed that few of the ten-thousand residents knew of this beautiful wilderness. In comparison, Purgatory Chasm, a short mile away, was usually bustling with a multi-faceted selection of humanity. Rowdy teenage boys, not yet convinced of their 'vincibility', dared each other to get closer to the edge of the eighty-foot drop into the crevasse. Cautious parents would climb along its boulder-strewn base, holding the hands of their younger children. Retiree birders would stroll Charley's loop around its perimeter, ever alert for a glimpse of scarlet tanagers.

Purgatory Chasm had an exhibit-filled ranger station, a covered gazebo for picnicking, and a playground carefully floored with shock-absorbing rubber.

Here, though, there was barely a wood sign-board to give one an idea of the lay of the land. The few reservoirs deep in the forest were marked, as well as where the forest proper overlapped with the Whitinsville Water Company property. That was it. Once you headed in here you were on your own. The maze of twisty little passages, all different, were as challenging to navigate as that classic Adventure game where you would be eaten by a grue once your lantern ran out of oil. A person new to the trails would be foolhardy to head in without a GPS or perhaps a pocket full of breadcrumbs.

In the full warmth of summer I would be alert to spot a few American toads, a scattering of dragonflies, and an attentive swarm of mosquitoes. This first day of November was both better and worse. The mosquitoes had long since departed, but along with them they had taken the amphibians and fluttering creatures that I usually delighted in on my walks. I had been rambling for a full hour now and the most I had heard was the plaintive *ank-ank* cry of a nuthatch. Maybe it, too, was wondering where the smaller tasty morsels had gone off to.

Still, with the trees now bare of their leafy cover, there was much to see. The woods were usually dense with foliage, making it hard to peer even a short distance into their depths. Now it was as if a bride had removed her veil and her beauty had been revealed. The edges of a ridge against the grey-blue sky showed a delicate tracery of granite amongst the darker stone. A stand of elderly oaks was stunning, the deep creases of the sand-brown bark rivaling the wise furrows in an aged grandfather's brow.

I came around a corner and stopped in surprise. A staggeringly tall oak had apparently succumbed to the storm's fury and had fallen diagonally across the path. A thick vine traced its way along the length of the tree, adding a beautiful spiraling pattern to the bark. The tree's crown stretched far into the brush on the left, but on the right the roots had been ripped up and a way was clear around them.

I moved off the trail to circumvent this interesting new obstacle in life, eyeing the tree. When I'd parked at the trail head there had been two trucks tucked along the roadside. One had been a crimson pick-up truck with no shotgun racks or other indications of hunting, at least that I could see. With luck the owner was just out for a walk like I was. The other vehicle had been a white F-150 clearly marked as belonging to the Department of Conservation. If the ranger was in here somewhere, hopefully he'd spotted the tree and was making plans to clear the trail. If I hadn't run into him by the time I emerged I'd leave him a note on his windshield.

My foot caught on a hidden root and I stumbled, catching myself against the rough bark of a mature oak. I shook my head, brushing my long, auburn hair back from my eyes. The forest floor was coated with perhaps two inches of oak leaves in tan, chocolate, fawn, and every other shade of brown I could imagine. My usual hunt for mushrooms had been stymied by the dense, natural carpet, and I knew better than to daydream while walking through this hazard.

My eyes moved up – and then stopped in surprise.

The elderly man lay on his back as if he had decided to take a mid-day nap during his stroll. His arms were spread, his head relaxing to one side. But his eyes were wide open, staring unfocused at the sky, long past seeing anything. The crimson blossom at his chest was a counterpoint to the dark green jacket he wore. The blood was congealed, the edges dry.

My hand went into my pocket before I gave it conscious thought, and then I was blowing sharply on the whistle I carried. It was only after a long minute that my mind began to clear from the shock, to give thought to the cell phone I carried in my other pocket. For so many years the whistle had been my first resort, the quickest way to communicate with fellow hikers.

I was just reaching into my other pocket when there was the whir and crunching of an approaching mountain bike. The ranger rode hard into view along the main trail, pulling to a skidding stop at the fallen tree. He was lean and well-built, perhaps a few years older than me, wearing a bright orange vest over a jacket peppered with foresting patches. His eyes swept me with concern.

"Are you hurt, miss?" he asked, his gaze sharp and serious as he caught his breath.

I found I could not speak, could only wave a hand in the direction of the fallen body. The dead man's hair was a pepper of grey amongst darker brown. He had been handsome, in a rough-hewn older cowboy sort of way, and in good shape for his age. Had he slipped on the leaves and fallen against a cut-off tree? Stiff and spindly stumps could almost seem like punji sticks, those sharp-edged spikes that the Viet-Cong laid as traps for unwary infantrymen.

The ranger gave a short shake of his head; I realized he could not see into the ravine from his vantage point. He climbed off his bike; his sure stride brought him to my side in seconds. He pulled up suddenly as his eyes caught sight of the body, then he slid down the slope, moving to kneel at the fallen man's side. He carefully laid a finger against the neck, pausing in silence, but I knew before he dropped his gaze what he would find.

He had his cell phone to his ear in moments, twisting loose the clasp on his bike helmet, running a hand through his thick, dark brown hair. "Jason here. We have a dead body in Sutton Woods, north of Melissa's Path. Just by where I reported that downed tree earlier. Get a team in here right away." He paused for a long moment, listening, his eyes sweeping the forest around him. "No," he responded shortly. "I think he's been –"

There was the shuffling of motion from above; both of us turned suddenly at the noise. A sinewy man stood there in day-glow orange, his wrinkled face speckled with age spots, a visored hunter's cap covering wisps of silvered hair. His eyes moved between the two of us with bright concern. "I heard the whistle. Is something wrong?"

In his hands he held a Ruger 10/22 rifle, the matte barrel pointed somewhere up-trail.

Jason settled into stillness. His eyes remained steady on the older man's, his lean frame solidifying somehow into a prepared crouch. The hand holding the phone gently eased down toward his hip. "Sir, I need to ask you to place your rifle on the ground and step back."

The hunter's worn brow creased in confusion. "I don't understand –"

"Sir," repeated Jason, a steely note sliding into his

request. "Put down the rifle." His hand was nearly at his hip now.

The hunter nodded, taking in the patches on Jason's shoulders, and lowered the rifle into the layer of leaves. When he stepped back, Jason moved with a speed I had not thought possible, putting himself between me and the hunter, taking up the rifle as if it was made of bamboo.

The hunter looked between us in surprise, and then his eyes drifted further, drawing in the sight below us. His face went white with shock and he staggered down to one knee. "My God! Is he dead?"

"Have you been shooting today?" asked Jason in response, moving his nose for a moment to the barrel of the gun to sniff for signs of firing.

"Yes, sure, for coyote," agreed the hunter, his voice rough. "But I'm careful! I never would've shot a *person*."

Jason glanced for a moment back at the fallen man. "He might not have been easy to see," he pointed out. "Forest green jacket, blue jeans, he could have looked like a shadowy movement."

The hunter shook his head fiercely. "Ask anyone," he stated, his voice becoming firmer. "I call them my Popovich Principles. I look three times before I even put my finger into the trigger guard. I hear too many tales of accidents. I only took three shots today, and each time my target was solid."

My throat was dry. "Were you sure of your background each time?"

He glanced up at me, and his brow creased even further. "I thought ... but I'm not sure ..."

Jason looked over to me, nodding. "We will figure

that all out soon enough," he agreed. "In the meantime, miss …"

"Morgan," I responded. "Morgan Warren. I live a few miles from here."

"Miss Warren," he echoed, an easing of tension releasing his shoulders. He rested the rifle butt-down on the forest floor. "If you don't mind, we can all wait here for the police and make sure we get all our facts straight."

I settled down cross-legged with my back against an aspen tree, breathing in the scent of juniper, and closed my eyes. After a few minutes a sense of calm resurfaced. The woods drifted toward the peaceful, quiet, eternal sense that it had possessed when I first stepped onto the trail only a short while ago.

* * *

The police had come and gone, the medics had respectfully carried away the dead body, and the forest had eased into a dark blue twilight that resembled the depths of an ocean floor. Jason had remained at my side through it all. Now he stared with me down at the empty space at the base of the ravine. The scattering of witch hazel along the edges added a faint golden glisten to the scene.

"But I didn't hear a shot," I stated finally, as if that made all the difference.

He gave his head a short shake. "Mr. Popovich began his hunting back at dawn," he pointed out. "The victim was apparently shot a few hours later. The body was long dead by the time you reached it. He was undoubtedly dead before you left your house to come here. The M.E. will let us know for sure."

"He looked asleep," I continued. My thoughts were

not quite coming in a coherent fashion.

He hesitated for a moment, then put an arm around my shoulder to comfort me. "Can I take you home?"

I shook my head. I was forty-three years old. Certainly old enough to be able to cope with this situation, as unusual as it was. And my home was a mere five-minute drive.

"I'll be fine," I assured him. But it was another long minute before I could pull my eyes from the spot and turn to navigate back around the fallen tree.

"We may need to ask you follow-up questions in the coming days, as we pursue our investigation," he murmured as we made our way up the trail.

"Of course," I agreed, my eyes taking in the forest around me as if it had recently sprung to life. Every twisted branch, every fluttering oak leaf clinging tenaciously to its tree sent a small surge of adrenaline through me. I wrapped my tangerine sarong even closer around my shoulders.

Worry creased Jason's eyes, and he ran a hand through his chestnut-brown hair. I wondered for a moment where his biking helmet had gone, and then remembered the police taking it and his bike back with them at his request.

A strange sense of loss nestled in my heart; I spoke to shake it loose. "I'm sorry to have kept you behind with me."

"Not at all," he demurred with understanding in his eyes. "I was happy to stay."

I lapsed into silence again, absorbed in the soft crunch of leaves beneath my feet, in the soft whistling of the dusk breeze as it scattered through birch and aspen. Jason was steady at my side. My shoulders slowly eased as we walked along the trail.

At last the trail widened before us. I'd never seen the vehicle gate at the mouth standing open, and it brought into focus again just what had happened here. I stared at it for a long moment before bringing my eyes up to the two cars standing side by side, his white F-150, my dark-green Forester.

He fished in a side pocket and brought out a card. "If you need anything – anything at all – you just call," he offered, and his eyes were warm as he handed the card to me.

I nodded, turned, and then I was back in the safety of my car, driving toward the security of home.

Here's where to learn what happened next!

Aspen Allegations

http://www.amazon.com/Aspen-Allegations-Sutton-Massachusetts-Mystery-ebook/dp/B00BO0K7ZI/

Thank you so much for all of your support and encouragement for this important cause.

Printed in Great Britain
by Amazon